SO YOU THINK YOU KNOW NARNIA?

Clive Gifford

*Hodder
Children's
Books*

a division of Hodder Headline Limited

© Hodder Children's Books 2005

Published in Great Britain in 2005
by Hodder Children's Books

Editor: Vic Parker
Design by Fiona Webb
Cover design: Hodder Children's Books

The right of Clive Gifford to be identified as the author of the work has been asserted by him in accordance with the Copyright, Designs and Patents Act 1988.

10 9 8 7 6 5 4 3 2 1

ISBN: 0 340 89392 3

Printed by Bookmarque Ltd, Croydon, Surrey

The paper and board used in this paperback by Hodder Children's Books are natural recyclable products made from wood grown in sustainable forests. The manufacturing processes conform to the environmental regulations of the country of origin.

Hodder Children's Books
a division of Hodder Headline Limited
338 Euston Road
London NW1 3BH

COVENTRY SCHOOLS' LIBRARY SERVICE

Please return this book on or before last date stamped.

SO YOU
THINK YOU
KNOW
NARNIA?

CONTENTS

INTRODUCTION

So you think you know all about Narnia, the magical happenings and creatures that live there? Think you can recall all of the battles, plots and voyages that occurred, the great feasts eaten, and the amazing characters and the friendships they made? Well this is the book for you. Contained in these pages are over 1,000 questions about the enchanted world – a few as simple as the donkey, Puzzle, but many as tough as a dwarf in battle. We hope you enjoy them.

About the author

Clive Gifford has never been to Narnia or met a unicorn or a faun. He does, however, have a wooden wardrobe not unlike the Professor's and can't help checking the back of it every now and then just in case. Deep in his heart, Clive knows that he's too old to visit Narnia and, besides, he's been too busy writing over 90 books for children including other titles in the 'So You Think You Know' series including *Roald Dahl*, *The Simpsons*, *Lemony Snicket* and *The Lord of the Rings*. Clive lives in Manchester and can be contacted through his website: www.clivegifford.co.uk.

EASY

QUESTIONS

1. Who wrote the Narnia books?

2. What sort of creature is Aslan?

3. Can you name either of the first two children to see Narnia?

4. The Pevensie children enter Narnia through what piece of furniture?

5. Which of these is a character in *The Magician's Nephew*: Uncle Albert, Uncle Andrew or Uncle Alan?

6. How many children are there in *The Lion, The Witch and The Wardrobe*?

7. Which king commanded a ship called the *Dawn Treader*?

8. Was Trumpkin: a dwarf, a faun or a mouse?

9. Can you name Lucy's sister and her two brothers?

10. How many books are there in the Narnia series: one, three, five or seven?

11. In which book do Polly and Digory first appear?

12. When Lucy, Susan and their brothers first enter Narnia, what season is it?

13. Which one of the following is not a book in the Narnia series: *The Magician's Nephew*, *The Voyage of the Dawn Treader*, *Aslan's Quest* or *The Last Battle*?

14. Are the talking animals of Narnia evil agents of the White Witch?

15. Can you name the only book in the series whose title does not begin with 'The'?

16. What was the colour of the sail on the ship, *Dawn Treader*?

17. In *The Last Battle*, what sort of creature was Puzzle?

18. Which is the only book in the Narnia series to include a type of relative in its title?

19. In *The Last Battle*, had King Tirian ever seen a lion before?

20. Where would you find Anvard castle: in Narnia, Calormen or Archenland?

21. Which one of the following is not a book in the Narnia series: *Prince Caspian, The Silver Chair* or *The Ice Queen*?

22. What was the name of the boy from Calormen who was the central character in *The Horse and his Boy*?

23. In *The Silver Chair*, who lives in Ettinsmoor: dwarfs, fauns or giants?

24. In *The Last Battle*, once Puzzle was shown to be a fake Aslan, lots of creatures of Narnia no longer believed in the real Aslan: true or false?

25. Where would you find Lantern Waste: in Narnia, Calormen or Archenland?

26. In *The Voyage of the Dawn Treader*, how many legs did the Duffers end up with?

27. In *The Silver Chair*, did Puddleglum have a gloomy, cheerful or angry personality?

28. Which of the following is not a character in the Narnia books: Jill, Polly or Ashley?

29. In which book did Jewel and Puzzle talk about grass, sugar, and looking after their hooves?

30. In *The Silver Chair*, what was the weather like when Eustace, Jill and Puddleglum reached Harfang: sunny, rainy or snowy?

31. In *The Last Battle*, who met his own father, King Erlian, at the golden gates: Tirian, Dorian or Frank?

32. Apart from sails, what other way could the *Dawn Treader* be moved?

33. Where is Tashbaan: in Narnia, Calormen or Archenland?

34. At the beginning of *The Magician's Nephew*, who climbs over the wall into Polly's back garden?

35. Uncle Andrew first offers Polly a ring of what colour?

36. In *The Horse and his Boy*, which Queen of Narnia did Shasta meet in Tashbaan: Susan, Lucy or Helen?

37. According to Puddleglum in *The Silver Chair*, are giants good shots when throwing things?

38. When Polly and Digory argue over hitting the golden bell, Digory grabs and hurts what part of Polly?

39. In *Prince Caspian*, which of the children had a pocket compass?

40. What sort of creature is Nikabrik: a dwarf, a faun or a leopard?

41. In *The Voyage of the Dawn Treader*, who turned Eustace from a dragon back into a boy?

42. What is Eustace's surname?

43. In *Prince Caspian*, Peter battles King Miraz. Who draws first blood?

44. In *Prince Caspian*, who challenges Trumpkin to a fencing match: Edmund or Eustace?

45. Who turns out to be Shasta's brother: Corin, Peter or Edmund?

46. In *Prince Caspian*, Aslan loathes Trumpkin: true or false?

47. Eustace learns to shoot a bow and arrow while voyaging on what boat?

48. In which book is there a Sunless Sea deep underground and a prince under a spell?

49. In *The Last Battle*, Shift insists that the squirrels of Narnia bring him large amounts of which food?

50. What sort of home do marsh-wiggles live in: huts, caves, reed boats or wig-wams?

MEDIUM QUESTIONS

QUIZ 1

1. In *The Voyage of the Dawn Treader*, whom does Prince Caspian leave as Regent of Narnia while he is away at sea: Duffle, Trumpkin or Griffle?

2. In *The Horse and his Boy*, the first faun Shasta ever meets has what name, beginning with T?

3. What is the name of the great castle on the eastern sea: Charn Castle, Cair Paravel or Auchen Fort?

4. In *The Last Battle*, High King Peter first introduces Tirian to whom: Queen Polly, Queen Lucy or King Edmund?

5. What does Mount Pire have at its top: a double peak, a single peak or a giant crater?

6. In *The Horse and his Boy*, what is the first talking animal Shasta meets in Narnia: an owl, a badger or a hedgehog?

7. In *The Magician's Nephew*, is Digory's father away in: Canada, India, Australia or Malaysia?

8. In *The Horse and his Boy*, when the Tisroc comes into a room for a secret meeting, Lasaraleen and Aravis hide behind what item of furniture?

9. In *Prince Caspian*, who is given the magic horn of Queen Susan?

10. In *The Horse and his Boy*, how many tombs are in the desert just outside the city of Tashbaan: half a dozen, a dozen or two dozen?

11. In *The Magician's Nephew*, a lady calls at Digory's house to give his mother: oranges, grapes, apples or chocolates?

12. In *The Voyage of the Dawn Treader*, which is the nearest of the Lone Islands: Doorn, Avra or Felimath?

13. In *The Lion, the Witch and the Wardrobe*, the Witch prepares to kill Edmund. What does the dwarf tie him to?

14. In *The Lion, the Witch and the Wardrobe*, which of the children had a sense of horror on hearing the name, Aslan?

15. What name did the animals of Narnia give Uncle Andrew because it was the word he muttered most often: Queen, Brandy, Cheat or Bounder?

16. *The Lion, the Witch and the Wardrobe* is set at the time of what twentieth-century conflict in our world?

17. Before Uncle Andrew tries using the rings with children, what sort of creature has he experimented on?

18. In *The Horse and his Boy*, where does Aslan meet Aravis and the horses: Cair Paravel, Anvard castle or the Hermit's house?

19. In *The Silver Chair*, when the owl was carrying Jill to meet Eustace and the other owls, what did he catch and eat in mid-air?

20. In *The Horse and his Boy*, a royal group want to escape secretly from Tashbaan. Someone has the idea of holding a banquet on-board their ship, to give them the opportunity. Who is this: Edmund, Shasta or Tumnus?

21. In *Prince Caspian*, which child challenges Trumpkin to an archery contest?

22. Mr Tumnus entertains Lucy by playing which musical instrument?

23. In *The Lion, the Witch and the Wardrobe*, which one of the following was a maid in the Professor's house: Ivy, Jackie or Lotty?

24. In *The Voyage of the Dawn Treader*, which Prince dives into the sea to help rescue Eustace, Edmund and Lucy?

25. What is the name of the first King of Narnia?

26. In *The Magician's Nephew*, who hit the gold bell to awaken the Queen?

27. In *The Horse and his Boy*, when Shasta was running in Archenland he met a king on a hunting trip. What was his name?

28. In the battle near the end of *The Lion, the Witch and the Wardrobe*, the Witch fought Peter with what weapon?

29. In *The Last Battle*, King Tirian wants Eustace and Jill to stay safe by going back to their own world, or where?

30. Uncle Andrew had a fairy godmother called Mrs Lefay. According to Mrs Lefay, which two other people also had fairy blood: a charwoman, a milkmaid, a princess or a duchess?

31. In *The Magician's Nephew*, what sort of fruit did Polly sometimes keep in her cash-box in the attic?

32. In *The Last Battle*, who cut King Tirian's cords with his pocket knife?

33. In *The Horse and his Boy*, what does Aslan say will happen to Rabadash if he strays more than ten miles from the great temple at Tashbaan?

34. When Lucy, Peter, Susan and Edmund first visit Narnia together, which is the first creature they follow: a robin, a jackdaw, a beaver or a squirrel?

35. In *Prince Caspian*, who gives Lucy back her bottle of magic cordial?

36. In *Prince Caspian*, who heals Trumpkin's painful wound just after the archery competition?

37. What is Aslan's How: a boat, a village, a mound or a lake?

38. In *The Lion, the Witch and the Wardrobe*, what item did Mr Tumnus carry to protect himself from the falling snow?

39. In *The Magician's Nephew*, the flying horse, Fledge, had wings which shone with which two colours: copper, silver, chestnut, bronze, slate?

40. In *The Horse and his Boy*, which one of the following was not a room in the Tisroc's palace: the Hall of Black Marble, the Hall of Pillars or the Hall of Ice?

41. Which faun told Lucy that he worked as a kidnapper for the White Witch?

42. Which creature used coins dropped by Uncle Andrew to fashion crowns for the new King and Queen of Narnia?

43. Shasta was caught in Tashbaan by lords from: Calormen, Narnia, Archenland or the Western Wilds?

44. When Shasta was close to the Tombs of the Ancient Kings, what cry was he scared by: a jackal's, a wolf's or a young girl's?

45. In *The Silver Chair*, what seasonal feast were the giants preparing for at Harfang castle?

46. Which one of the four children from *The Lion, the Witch and the Wardrobe* was no longer interested in Narnia by the time of *The Last Battle*?

47. When Lucy, Edmund and Eustace arrived on the *Dawn Treader*, how many days had it been sailing: nearly 14, nearly 30 or nearly 60 days?

48. In *The Lion, the Witch and the Wardrobe*, the children found a note at Mr Tumnus's ransacked cave. In it, which one of the following was the White Witch not called: Empress of the Lone Islands, High Ruler of Narnia or Imperial Majesty Queen Jadis?

49. In *Prince Caspian*, Aslan tells Peter and Susan that they won't be returning to Narnia, and later, neither will Edmund and Lucy. Why?

50. In *The Lion, the Witch and the Wardrobe*, Susan was attacked at the Stone Table by what sort of creature: a centaur, a giant or a wolf?

QUIZ 2

1. In *The Magician's Nephew*, Aslan gives some animals the power to talk. How many of each type of animal does he pick?

2. In *The Silver Chair*, what emotion did Jill and Eustace see on the faces of the Earthmen in Underland: anger, glee, surprise or sadness?

3. Who betrayed his three brothers and sisters by heading off to see the Queen?

4. Who did Ramandu's daughter marry, at the end of *The Voyage of the Dawn Treader*?

5. In *The Last Battle*, Tirian rescues a group of creatures being sent to Calormen to: tin mines, salt mines or copper mines?

6. In *The Last Battle*, Farsight saw a close ally of King Tirian dead from a Calormen arrow in his side. Who was this?

7. Which character in *The Horse and his Boy* could not read or write: Shasta, Corin, Aravis or Lord Darrin?

8. Who made two copies of the magical map of the voyage of the *Dawn Treader*: Coriakin, Aslan or Caspian?

9. Which of the four children in *Prince Caspian* was the only one to enter Narnia without a coat?

10. At the start of *The Last Battle*, what was the name of the old ape?

11. In *Prince Caspian*, what sort of animal is Hogglestock?

12. In Uncle Andrew's study, what colour was the tray on which the magic rings were placed?

13. In *The Horse and his Boy*, what part of Shasta's body was bandaged after the battle: his chest, his head, his hand or his foot?

14. The Tombs of the Ancient Kings is first mentioned in which book: *The Horse and his Boy*, *The Last Battle* or *The Magician's Nephew*?

15. When Lasaraleen helped Aravis sneak out of Tashbaan, what did Aravis pretend to be?

16. In *Prince Caspian*, which one of the children had an arrow hit their helmet when trekking from Glasswater Creek?

17. Did the White Witch tell Edmund that she was: Empress of Auchenland, Queen of Narnia or Watcher of the Skies?

18. In *Prince Caspian*, who was the second child able to see Aslan?

19. In *The Silver Chair*, who burst into tears at the sight of the Queen and King and the other giants at Harfang: Lucy, Jill, Susan or Eustace?

20. In *The Voyage of the Dawn Treader*, who was immediately seasick on the ship: Edmund, Lucy or Eustace?

21. In *The Lion, the Witch and the Wardrobe*, who fought and killed the wolf which attacked Susan at the Stone Table?

22. According to Mr Tumnus, do nymphs live in: forests, wells, caves or swamps?

23. In *Prince Caspian*, who shot the bear which attacked Lucy in the woods?

24. In *The Silver Chair*, who was talking about rocks looking like giants when the rocks turned out to be giants?

25. Who smashed the silver chair with his sword?

26. Who warns Prince Caspian that he is in danger from his uncle?

27. In *The Magician's Nephew*, what is the name of the Queen, also called the Witch? It begins with J.

28. In *The Horse and his Boy*, which King of Narnia did Shasta meet in Tashbaan?

29. Which creature took Shasta's message to Queen Lucy: a stag, an eagle or a horse?

30. At the start of *Prince Caspian*, at what sort of building do we find Peter, Lucy, Susan and Edmund?

31. In *The Voyage of the Dawn Treader*, what weapon did the Sea King shake at Lucy: a spear, a sword, a walrus's tusk or an axe?

32. In *The Voyage of the Dawn Treader*, who made Lord Bern a Duke of the Lone Islands?

33. What did Edmund think about having, on his way to the Queen of Narnia's house: a private cinema, a swimming pool or a giant storehouse of Turkish Delight?

34. In *The Voyage of the Dawn Treader*, what held Coriakin's magic book shut: two clasps, a lock or stout rope?

35. What was the first brave thing that Eustace did on the *Dawn Treader*'s voyage: attack a sea serpent with a sword, fight a live dragon, or imprison Governor Gumpas?

36. In *The Silver Chair*, as Eustace and the others crossed an arched bridge over the river, how many horseriders did they see?

37. Where did Prince Caspian's forces first fight Miraz's armies: the Dancing Lawn, Aslan's How, or Lantern Waste?

38. In the Scrubbs' house, what was the subject of the picture which started moving?

39. Miraz was a kind and generous ruler of Narnia: true or false?

40. What musical instrument did Old Father Time use to call the stars in from Narnia?

41. In *The Silver Chair*, the boat which Jill and the others travelled on in Underland was driven by: steam, a sail or oars?

42. Who laid on a tournament for Prince Caspian: the Duke of Calormen, the Duke of Galma, or the Duke of Archenland?

43. In *The Horse and his Boy*, was Arsheesh: a farmer, a baker, a fisherman or a poet?

44. In *The Last Battle*, who picked some violets to try to convince the dwarfs that they were no longer in the stable?

45. In *Prince Caspian*, what was the name of the creek that the four children and Trumpkin rowed up and made a camp alongside?

46. Who made some guinea pigs explode when experimenting with magic dust?

47. Which three children suddenly found themselves drawn through a picture into the sea?

48. In *The Silver Chair*, the giants at Harfang give Jill a bright robe to wear. What colour is it?

49. In *The Voyage of the Dawn Treader*, what is the name of the leader of the slave traders in the Lone Islands: Pug, Tack or Drong?

50. Who killed Prince Caspian's father?

QUIZ 3

1. In *Prince Caspian*, which two of the children does Aslan say will not be returning to Narnia again?

2. Who does Aravis first tell that Bree and Hwin are talking horses: Queen Susan, King Edmund or Lasaraleen?

3. When Aslan returns after being killed at the Stone Table, what has happened to his mane: it is missing, it has regrown, it has been replaced by a helmet?

4. In *The Lion, the Witch and the Wardrobe*, how far is the old Professor's house from the nearest post office: two, four, six or eight miles?

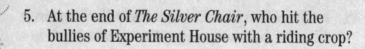

5. At the end of *The Silver Chair*, who hit the bullies of Experiment House with a riding crop?

6. In *The Silver Chair*, what is the name of the owl who introduces Jill and Eustace to Trumpkin: Oswald the Wise, Sagewings or Glimfeather?

7. In *Prince Caspian*, where does Pattertwig manage to get dozens of fauns to arrive: the Dancing Lawn, the Lantern Waste, Beruna Ford or Cair Paravel?

8. In *The Voyage of the Dawn Treader*, which prince is sold by a slave trader for 150 crescents?

9. At the end of *The Magician's Nephew*, what do Polly and Digory do with all the magic rings: bury them, burn them or sell them?

10. In *The Voyage of the Dawn Treader*, where do Caspian and the others meet the dragon: in the woods, at sea or on the beach?

11. In *The Magician's Nephew*, Aslan tells Digory to head to a land west of Narnia called: the Western Badlands, the Western Wild or the West Archenland Plateau?

12. A giant member of Prince Caspian's army blunders at their biggest battle, near Aslan's How. Who is this?

13. In *Prince Caspian*, the children equip Trumpkin from the treasure store at Cair Paravel. Which one of the following items was he not given: a helmet, a shield, an axe, a bow?

14. When the water barrels were leaking on the *Dawn Treader*, how much water was each person limited to per day: two pints, one pint or half a pint?

15. In *The Voyage of the Dawn Treader*, what do Caspian and the others eat on their first night on Dragon Island: roasted pig, roasted goat, fruits and berries, or dried nuts?

16. In *Prince Caspian*, who tells Lucy to wake the other children and Trumpkin and to get them to follow: Aslan, Miraz, Trufflehunter or Tirian?

17. As they sailed towards the end of the world, what sort of white flower did those on the *Dawn Treader* spot in the water?

18. What sort of creature decorated the shield given to Peter in *The Lion, the Witch and The Wardrobe*?

19. In which book did Lucy learn the thoughts of Marjorie Preston and Anne Featherstone after uttering a spell?

20. Are we told that Eustace's school is a boys-only school or that it is mixed?

21. What type of food is pavenders: fruit, fish, vegetables, or spiced cakes?

22. In *The Voyage of the Dawn Treader*, after Eustace had been a dragon, did he become more or less rude and annoying?

23. In *The Lion, the Witch and the Wardrobe*, where are Lucy and Mr Tumnus reunited: at the Stone Table, in Cair Paravel, or at the Witch's house?

24. In *The Silver Chair*, the Lady of the Green Kirtle told Jill and the others to head to which castle?

25. What was the sun in Charn like compared to our sun: smaller and more yellow, or bigger and more red?

26. In *Prince Caspian*, who did Glozelle stab to death in the back: Peter, Reepicheep, Miraz, or Trufflehunter?

27. Who did Aslan command to shut the doorway out of Narnia: Tirian, Peter, Eustace or Digory?

28. Can you name two of the four creatures who sat with Prince Caspian when he decided to blow Susan's horn?

29. What did Lucy, Peter, Susan and Edmund discover in the long room full of pictures in the Professor's house: a wardrobe, a suit of armour or a map of Narnia?

30. In *The Voyage of the Dawn Treader*, what colour was the hair of the Sea People?

31. What food did the Queen of Narnia give Edmund, which he found very addictive?

32. In *The Voyage of the Dawn Treader*, Eustace the dragon took a long drink at a pool then, shockingly, ate what creature?

33. In *The Last Battle*, where were Eustace and Jill when they suddenly found a way into Narnia: on a train, in their school grounds or visiting an English castle?

34. Before Puddleglum, Eustace and Jill set out for Ettinsmoor, what large piece of meat did Puddleglum roll up inside their blankets?

35. What happens if the Deplorable Word is spoken?

36. In *The Last Battle*, King Tirian first caught a glimpse of the creature pretending to be Aslan at what hill?

37. In *The Last Battle*, what instrument did Rishda's forces use to summon up reinforcements?

38. In *The Last Battle*, after walking through the golden gates, which queen was sitting on a throne at the foot of a tree with a phoenix: Queen Susan, Queen Helen or Queen Lucy?

39. In *The Horse and his Boy*, what was the second creature that Shasta met in Narnia: a hedgehog, a badger or a rabbit?

40. In *The Lion, the Witch and the Wardrobe*, what sort of creature is Rumblebuffin: a giant, a centaur, a faun or a dwarf?

41. In *The Magician's Nephew*, a horse travelled with Digory, Polly and the others into a new world. What was its fruity name?

42. What creature walks beside Shasta as he heads to Anvard?

43. In *The Lion, the Witch and the Wardrobe*, who led Lucy back from the cave to the lamp post?

44. What was the name of Prince Caspian's evil uncle?

45. In *Prince Caspian*, which one of the children breaks their pocket knife by clearing the ivy away from the door at Cair Paravel?

46. In *The Silver Chair*, Puddleglum is caught by the giants' hunting party: true or false?

47. In *The Magician's Nephew*, the talking rabbit thought that Digory and the other humans were what sort of vegetable?

48. In *Prince Caspian*, who had the title, 'Duke of Lantern Waste and Count of the Western March'?

49. In *The Silver Chair*, Eustace slipped a gold bracelet from the dragon's treasure hoard onto which arm – his left or right?

50. What sort of weapon does Reepicheep wear?

QUIZ 4

1. What sort of creature is Mr Tumnus?

2. What colour is the White Witch's wand: golden, silver or black?

3. According to *The Magician's Nephew*, what did the second son of Queen Helen and King Frank become: King of Narnia, King of Archenland, King of the Western Wild or King of the Southern Mountains?

4. In *The Lion, the Witch and the Wardrobe*, which one of the following was not a creature the Queen called to battle: the Cruels, the Hags, the Spectres or the Trolls?

5. Can you name any of the three Lords sleeping an enchanted sleep in front of a giant banquet in *The Voyage of the Dawn Treader*?

6. In *The Silver Chair*, Jill and Eustace are to be served as part of the giants' feast between the joint and what other course?

7. In *The Lion, the Witch and the Wardrobe*, who promised Mr Beaver that the leaks at his dam would be fixed by the time he returned?

8. In *The Horse and his Boy*, which two boys rode at the very back of the army of Narnia who were to go into battle against Prince Rabadash's forces?

9. In *The Lion, the Witch and the Wardrobe*, what happened to the Stone Table after Aslan reappeared?

10. In the combat between Peter and Miraz in *Prince Caspian*, Glenstorm the centaur was a marshal: true or false?

11. What is Mr Ketterley's first name?

12. In *The Lion, the Witch and the Wardrobe*, who rode on Aslan's back to the Witch's home?

13. The Duffers were renamed Monopods but got their names mixed up. What did they end up calling themselves?

14. In *The Silver Chair*, who had too much of the giants' liquor on their first evening in Harfang?

15. In *The Last Battle*, who did the god, Tash, seize inside the stable: Tirian, Rishda or the ape?

16. In *The Voyage of the Dawn Treader*, who was granted his greatest wish of untroubled sleep on Star Island?

17. What was the name of the castle which was the home of Peter, Susan, Lucy and Edmund when they ruled Narnia?

18. In *The Lion, the Witch and the Wardrobe*, when sightseers came to the Professor's house, who showed them around: Mrs Macready, the Professor, Ivy the maid, or the children?

19. In *Prince Caspian*, what kind of creature was Lilygloves: a mole, a centaur, a leopard or a faun?

20. In *Prince Caspian*, what was the name of the river in which Edmund first sees Aslan?

21. In *The Lion, the Witch and the Wardrobe*, can you name two out of the following list of creatures sent to rescue Edmund from the Queen: unicorns, cheetahs, harpies, deer?

22. In *Prince Caspian*, who does Lucy say is urging the others to go up the gorge rather than down?

23. What was the Splendour Hyaline: a magic flower, a ship or a festival in honour of Aslan?

24. In *The Voyage of the Dawn Treader*, what colour was Ramandu's daughter dressed in?

25. In *The Silver Chair*, what was the name of the gnome captured by Puddleglum: Golg, Bism, Mave or Forg?

26. In *The Silver Chair*, where did Jill, Eustace and Puddleglum meet the Black Knight for the second time: in Harfang Castle, in Narnia or in Underland?

27. What sort of vehicle did Uncle Andrew hire for Queen Jadis: a hansom cab, a hot air balloon, a sedan chair or a flying carpet?

28. Where is Lantern Waste: Narnia, London, Archenland or the Wood Between the Worlds?

29. Shasta had never before seen which common breakfast item in Narnia: a boiled egg, sausages, or toast?

30. In *The Silver Chair*, Jill entered Narnia wearing which two of the following: a blazer, a raincoat, a sweater, a summer dress?

31. Which word describes an important lady in Calormen: Tarken, Tarkheena, Caloren or Caloreena?

32. In *The Last Battle*, when Tirian attacked enemies at Stable Hill, which type of talking animal rushed to his aid?

33. In *Prince Caspian*, Caspian and his tutor watched the planets at night from where: the Great Central Tower, the Western Tower or the Eastern Battlements?

34. In *Prince Caspian*, Lucy uses her bottle of magic cordial to heal Reepicheep, but what part of him remains missing?

35. What does Jill call Eustace throughout most of *The Silver Chair*: Eustie, Snooty or Scrubb?

36. In *Prince Caspian*, which two children rowed the boat towards Glasswater Creek?

37. In *Prince Caspian*, what kind of squirrel is Pattertwig: a grey squirrel, a red squirrel or a striped black and white squirrel?

38. When Prince Caspian fled his uncle's castle, which one of the following did he not carry with him: venison slices, some wine, his sword, a compass, some bread?

39. When Polly and Digory were with the Queen in Charn, how many stars near the sun could they see?

40. In *The Magician's Nephew*, who slept amongst her ancestors in the Hall of Images for a thousand years?

41. In *The Voyage of the Dawn Treader*, what was the black thing that Lucy saw at the bottom of the sea: a shark, a sea serpent or the *Dawn Treader*'s shadow?

42. In *The Voyage of the Dawn Treader*, what did the invisible people do: torture Caspian, feed everyone, or imprison them all?

43. In *Prince Caspian*, Glenstorm the centaur has how many sons?

44. In *The Horse and his Boy*, as King Lune's party ride their horses back to Anvard, who gets left behind?

45. What is the full name of the heroine in *The Magician's Nephew*?

46. In *The Voyage of the Dawn Treader*, the Magician spotted the Duffers washing up the plates before dinner, to save time after dinner: true or false?

47. In *Prince Caspian*, who kills the Hag at Aslan's How?

48. How far was the waterfall at Beaversdam from Miraz's castle: a mile, 10 miles, 100 miles, or 500 miles?

49. In *The Lion, the Witch and the Wardrobe*, when Mr and Mrs Beaver and the children left the dam, who walked immediately behind the leader, Mr Beaver?

50. Jadis says that magic is only found in people: with cold blue eyes, with royal blood, or with great wealth?

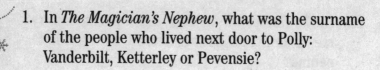

1. In *The Magician's Nephew*, what was the surname of the people who lived next door to Polly: Vanderbilt, Ketterley or Pevensie?

2. In *Prince Caspian*, what was the only weapon that Trumpkin carried on his journey to Cair Paravel?

3. In *The Lion, the Witch and the Wardrobe*, who thinks Lucy came from the great city of War Drobe?

4. Which friend did Caspian nearly kill with an axe on hearing that his son had vanished?

5. According to Eustace in *The Voyage of the Dawn Treader*, what food does a dragon most like: fresh goat, fresh humans, fresh dragon or fresh mice?

6. When the Pevensie children reached Mr Tumnus's cave, what had happened to the picture of Mr Tumnus's father?

7. In *The Voyage of the Dawn Treader*, which was the first talking animal that Eustace saw: a beaver, a horse or a mouse?

8. In *The Magician's Nephew*, who threw Aunt Letty across the room of her house in London?

9. When Lucy met Edmund in Narnia for the first time, what meal had she just had with Mr Tumnus?

10. In *The Horse and his Boy*, who was the one member of the Calormen forces who was captured and held in Archenland?

11. In *The Last Battle*, who did the dwarfs not believe in, even when he appeared in front of them and gave them a great feast?

12. In *The Lion, the Witch and the Wardrobe*, Aslan showed someone the lands they would rule over as king in the future. Who was this?

13. In *The Last Battle*, whose great-grandfather's great-grandfather was King Rilian, who featured in *The Silver Chair*?

14. Shasta first mentioned the talking horse to whom: Prince Corin, Queen Susan or King Edmund?

15. In *The Silver Chair*, why did Jill and the others stop eating the cold venison served by the giants for lunch?

16. Was the Old Raven of Ravenscaur a friend or an enemy of Prince Caspian?

17. In *The Voyage of the Dawn Treader*, who is asked to cast a magic spell to make the invisible people visible again?

18. What was the strange name of Jill and Eustace's school, mentioned in *The Silver Chair*?

19. In *The Horse and his Boy*, what bird's song did Shasta hear for the very first time: a robin, a nightingale, a thrush or a lark?

20. In *The Voyage of the Dawn Treader*, which child did Reepicheep repeatedly stab with his rapier?

21. In *The Horse and his Boy*, who was hurt by a lion's attack: Bree, Hwin, Shasta or Aravis?

22. In *The Last Battle*, how many dwarfs did Rishda's forces capture: seven, 11 or 15?

23. What was the name of the pool from which Puzzle fished out the lion skin?

24. In *Prince Caspian*, who sent a challenge to Miraz for single combat?

25. In *The Silver Chair*, what was the name of the castle that Jill and Eustace spotted as soon as they entered Narnia?

26. Susan was best at which two of the following activities: horseriding, archery, swimming, chess, climbing?

27. What common pet did Polly and Digory see with a ring tied round its middle with tape?

28. How many hags did the White Witch command to bind Aslan at the Stone Table?

29. What was the name of the place Aravis and Shasta planned to meet after they had got through the city of Tashbaan?

30. Who received a new sewing machine from Father Christmas?

31. What happened to the sun as the *Dawn Treader* sailed nearer and nearer to the end of the world?

32. How many falls did Bree say Shasta had on his first day of riding: one, half a dozen, a dozen or two dozen?

33. Did Shasta see a stream grow out of Aslan's tears or Aslan's footprint?

34. When Shift the ape dressed himself up in clothes, what colour was his jacket?

35. In *The Silver Chair*, what was the first animal who talked to Jill and Eustace in Narnia: a badger, a mouse or an owl?

36. What fell after Digory had hit the golden bell: part of the roof, some chandeliers, or a throne?

37. In *The Lion, the Witch and the Wardrobe*, where did Aslan, the children and their army camp: the Secret Hill, the Cair River or the Fords of Beruna?

38. Where did Digory, Polly and Jadis arrive when they returned back to London: in Polly's bedroom, in Digory's garden or in Uncle Andrew's study?

39. In which season of the year does *The Last Battle* begin?

40. What did Susan become known in Narnia as: Queen Susan the Kind, Queen Susan the Gentle or Queen Susan the Wise?

41. When Polly and Digory left the Wood between the Worlds and arrived in a crumbling palace, what did they find hundreds of: statues, elves, wolves or lions?

42. In *The Last Battle*, when King Tirian had a dream in Lantern Waste, how many human beings did he see?

43. In *The Voyage of the Dawn Treader*, what creature is Eustace turned into?

44. In *The Last Battle*, what did Jill think was the most beautiful creature she had ever seen?

45. In *The Magician's Nephew*, the Cabby and his horse entered the new world with Polly and the others: true or false?

46. In *The Lion, the Witch and the Wardrobe*, where did the Queen most want to kill Edmund: in her home, at the Stone Table, at Cair Paravel or by the lamp post?

47. In *The Horse and his Boy*, what colour was Anradin's beard dyed: blue, gold, crimson or purple?

48. What were the statues of people in the palace at Charn dressed in: rags, fine robes or suits of armour?

49. What game were the four Pevensie children playing when Lucy entered the wardrobe and Narnia for the second time?

50. In *Prince Caspian*, who was chained to Beruna Bridge: the river-god, a nymph, Trufflehunter or Aslan?

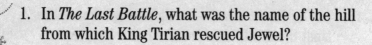

1. In *The Last Battle*, what was the name of the hill from which King Tirian rescued Jewel?

2. In *The Last Battle*, what sort of creature was Ginger?

3. In *Prince Caspian*, which one of the children said that they once fought a battle at Beruna?

4. In *The Lion, the Witch and the Wardrobe*, when Edmund reached the Queen's house, what was the first statue he saw: a statue of a wolf, a statue of a lion, or a statue of a small boy?

5. Which creature in Narnia thought that Uncle Andrew was a tree: the ox, the warthog, the raven or the jackdaw?

6. In *The Horse and his Boy*, when visiting the Kings and Queens of Narnia, had Prince Rabadash been: charming, unpleasant, or too shy to speak?

7. In *Prince Caspian*, what type of creature are the Seven Brothers of Shuddering Wood?

8. In *The Last Battle*, what creature sniffed out the scent of a Calormen soldier after the old land of Narnia had ended?

9. In *The Last Battle*, Eustace and Jill disguise themselves as soldiers from which land?

10. In *The Silver Chair*, as Jill escaped from Underland, what dance was being performed by dwarfs?

11. In *Prince Caspian*, which child is the first to see Aslan?

12. At the beginning of *The Last Battle*, the last of the Kings of Narnia sat under what type of tree?

13. In *Prince Caspian*, was Glenstorm: a warrior, a prophet, a musician, or a magician?

14. In *Prince Caspian*, which mouse was seriously injured in the battle with Miraz's forces?

15. In *The Magician's Nephew*, how many river-nymphs held the Queen of Narnia's train during her coronation: two, four, 12 or 40?

16. In *The Horse and his Boy*, what sort of weapon do the Calormen forces use to try to knock down the gates of Anvard castle?

17. In *The Silver Chair*, to which land did Aslan blow Eustace to when he fell off the cliff?

18. Who performed some magic to cause Prince Caspian's gentlemen-in-waiting to fall asleep?

19. Who put her arm around Puzzle's neck and pleaded with King Tirian not to kill him?

20. Shasta met a red dwarf in Narnia. What was his name: Snuffle, Truffle or Duffle?

21. In *The Last Battle*, what was the name of the hill on which a bonfire was lit each night?

22. In *The Voyage of the Dawn Treader*, can you name two of the four characters who sailed in the coracle towards the end of the world?

23. Who had four cousins called Peter, Susan, Edmund and Lucy?

24. In *The Voyage of the Dawn Treader*, what name, beginning with the letter D, does the Magician give to the invisible people on the island?

25. What was the name of the giant from Deadman's Hill who joined Prince Caspian's army?

26. Uncle Andrew put on his best clothes after meeting Jadis. What colour was his waistcoat?

27. Where does the Queen tell Edmund that her home lies: between two lakes, between two hills, or between two cliffs?

28. Which prince fought with Thornbut, the dwarf, because he was not allowed into battle?

29. How many mice does Reepicheep say are at Prince Caspian's command: six, 12 or 24?

30. In *The Voyage of the Dawn Treader*, which one of the four Pevensie children went to America with their parents?

31. Which of the children receives an ivory horn from Father Christmas?

32. What jewel was set in the crown of King Frank of Narnia?

33. After Aravis said goodbye to Lasaraleen at the water-gate, what sort of transport did she use: a punt, a canoe or a yacht?

34. Why did the Queen's sledge start to travel more slowly as she pursued Lucy, Susan and Peter?

35. In *The Voyage of the Dawn Treader*, when did the Duffers wake up from their sleep: one o'clock, three o'clock or five o'clock?

36. In *The Horse and his Boy*, what or who was Azim Balda: an evil lord, a sacred mountain, or a city?

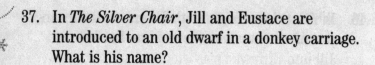

37. In *The Silver Chair*, Jill and Eustace are introduced to an old dwarf in a donkey carriage. What is his name?

38. In *The Magician's Nephew*, who are we told had fairy blood: Miss Ketterley, Mrs Plummer or Mrs Lefay?

39. In *The Last Battle*, which former child in a Narnia book does Eustace call the 'Professor'?

40. Which orphan boy in a Narnia story reappears in a later tale as the King of Archenland?

41. In *The Lion, the Witch and the Wardrobe*, Edmund drew two things on a statue of a lion. Can you name either of them?

42. In *The Last Battle*, which child was thrown into the stable by a Calormen soldier?

43. Which court was Lord Darrin a member of: the court of Archenland, the court of Calormen, or the court of Narnia?

44. In *The Last Battle*, was Swanwhite: a unicorn, an ancient Queen of Narnia, or a baby faun?

45. In *The Magician's Nephew*, who did Digory give the apple of life to?

46. In *The Silver Chair*, the owls say that the only sort of creature which can guide Eustace and Jill into Ettinsmoor is what?

47. In *The Lion, the Witch and the Wardrobe*, who warned the Queen of the possible arrival of Aslan: Maugrim, Mr Tumnus or Edmund?

48. What was the name of the faun that Lucy encountered the first time she stepped through the wardrobe?

49. In *The Voyage of the Dawn Treader*, who was the first to spot invisible enemies on the island ruled by Coriakin?

50. How long did Polly and Digory's adventures in Narnia take back in London: an hour, a day, a week or almost no time at all?

QUIZ 7

1. When Wimbleweather first arrived at Prince Caspian's camp, what creatures did he carry in a basket?

2. In *The Voyage of the Dawn Treader*, how did Lord Rhoop feel at meeting Caspian: delighted, scared or very angry?

3. Who managed to break the Witch's wand during the great battle in *The Lion, the Witch and the Wardrobe*?

4. When the hermit nursed Aravis, what animal's milk did he give her?

5. In *The Lion, the Witch and the Wardrobe*, which two children talk to the Professor over their fears for Lucy's health?

6. In *The Silver Chair*, who stood on Puddleglum's shoulders to be the first out of Underland?

7. In which month of the year did King Caspian's wife die?

8. In *The Horse and his Boy*, who turned Rabadash into an animal?

9. According to *The Last Battle*, when has Tirian been to the Tisroc's court: as a baby, as a child, as an adult, or never?

10. According to CS Lewis, how much is a crescent worth in British money: about a quarter of a British pound, about a third of a British pound, or about half a British pound?

11. In Narnia, how often are unicorns used like horses to ride on: never or frequently?

12. The Tisroc, the Grand Vizier and Prince Rabadash were accompanied by how many deaf and dumb slaves?

13. In *The Last Battle*, Rishda says that if the talking dogs surrender, they will be housed in whose kennels?

14. When Mr Tumnus first met Lucy, what colour muffler was he wearing?

15. Who claimed the title of Chatelaine of Cair Paravel: Queen Jadis, Aslan, Peter, or the Professor?

16. Edmund received a giant train set from Father Christmas: true or false?

17. In *The Last Battle*, who says that Aslan cannot be bothered to talk to alot of stupid talking animals: King Tirian, Puzzle or Shift?

18. In *The Last Battle*, a Calormen soldier dares to go into the stable at Stable Hill to see the god, Tash. What is his name?

19. In *The Silver Chair*, who is sorely tempted to take a trip to the land of Bism, but convinced otherwise by Puddleglum?

20. In *The Horse and his Boy*, what was Rogin: a centaur, a dwarf or a faun?

21. In *The Last Battle*, a talking mouse wearing a red-feathered circlet on his head meets Lucy, Tirian and the others at the golden gates. What is his name?

22. In *The Horse and his Boy*, what is the name of the stag who carries the message of Rabadash's invasion to King Edmund: Sallowpad, Rogin or Chervy?

23. In *The Voyage of the Dawn Treader*, the feast at Aslan's Table had pies shaped like elephants and dragons: true or false?

24. In *The Last Battle*, the children give King Tirian three kinds of sandwich to eat. Can you name two of them?

25. In *The Magician's Nephew*, Polly and Digory first arrived in what part of the palace: the courtyard, the dungeons, the ballroom or the high tower?

26. Which character does Lucy go to tea with during her first visit to Narnia?

27. Which two of the Pevensie children saw the Witch just before she killed Aslan?

28. In *The Silver Chair*, according to the giants' cookbook, what creature can be stringy and have a muddy flavour: venison, faun, marsh-wiggle or centaur?

29. Who called the city of Charn the wonder of the world: the Queen, Digory or Polly?

30. In *The Lion, the Witch and the Wardrobe*, the robin led the four children to what creature: a beaver, a wolf, a dwarf or a faun?

31. In *Prince Caspian*, when the children arrived in Narnia, where did they first find themselves: at a thicket, at a well, at a cave, or at the top of a hill?

32. At the beginning of *The Silver Chair*, who does Eustace tell of his time in other worlds?

33. After Digory met the Witch at the silver apple tree, which compass direction did she head off in?

34. In which book was Wild Fresney cooked, along with wood pigeons, to make a meal?

35. Who once served marmalade roll at a meal in Narnia: Mr Tumnus, Aslan, Prince Caspian, or Mr and Mrs Beaver?

36. In *The Horse and his Boy*, how long was the beard of the Hermit of the Southern March: almost to his chest, almost to his waist, almost to his knees?

37. Where were Hwin and Aravis planning to head when they first met Shasta?

38. In *The Voyage of the Dawn Treader*, what colour were the eyes of the dragon that Eustace saw?

39. In *The Lion, the Witch and the Wardrobe*, when the children reach the Stone Table, which one of the following creatures is not with Aslan: a pelican, a unicorn, a tiger or four centaurs?

40. Polly was sent to bed as punishment for playing with Digory and coming home late – but for how many hours?

41. In *The Voyage of the Dawn Treader*, when Eustace became a dragon, what was his main emotion: anger, delight or loneliness?

42. In *The Silver Chair*, the giants at Harfang gave Eustace a tunic and cloak of what colour?

43. In *The Voyage of the Dawn Treader*, who was the first to spot that the dragon was shedding hot tears: Lucy, Edmund or Reepicheep?

44. In *Prince Caspian*, who steered the boat to Glasswater Creek?

45. What board game did Lucy and Reepicheep play on-board the *Dawn Treader*?

46. In *The Lion, the Witch and the Wardrobe*, what did Rumblebuffin use to knock down the gates of the Witch's house?

47. In *Prince Caspian*, what was the name of the dwarf who was killed in the fight inside the mound at Aslan's How?

48. In *The Lion, the Witch and the Wardrobe*, which of the children feels brave and full of adventure at the first mention of the name, Aslan?

49. Susan received two gifts from Father Christmas. When she returned to Narnia in *Prince Caspian*, which did she not find at Cair Paravel?

50. In *The Silver Chair*, who stamped his foot on the Queen's fire in order to help break the enchantment?

1. In *The Voyage of the Dawn Treader*, what was the name of the Lord who bought Caspian at the slave market?

2. In *The Horse and his Boy*, the Tisroc fears that one of his sons might rise up against him in the near future. What is this son's name?

3. In *The Silver Chair*, after the Queen of Underland's spell failed, what creature did she turn into?

4. In which book was Narnia always in winter, never reaching Christmas?

5. In *The Lion, the Witch and the Wardrobe*, who was the eldest child?

6. In *The Voyage of the Dawn Treader*, what was the name of the old man at World's End: Endor, Ramandu or Catkin?

7. In *The Last Battle*, who told the creatures at Stable Hill that a donkey had dressed up as Aslan: Rishda, Shift or Edmund?

8. In *The Silver Chair*, what is the name of King Caspian's son who is missing?

9. In *Prince Caspian*, what jewels were in the eyes of the knight chess piece?

10. Who met Shasta, sporting a black eye and missing a tooth?

11. In *The Voyage of the Dawn Treader*, when Eustace had found he was lying on prickly things in the dragon's cave, what did they turn out to be: thorns, claws, or gold crowns?

12. In *Prince Caspian*, according to Peter, what type of people was Pomona the greatest of: the water-people, the desert-people or the wood-people?

13. When Lucy opened the wardrobe for the first time, what fell out: two mothballs, a coat hanger, a scarf, or a troll?

14. In *Prince Caspian*, what important landmark from *The Lion, the Witch and the Wardrobe* is found at the centre of Aslan's How?

15. What was the name of the little white town on the island of Doorn?

16. What sort of creature did the Sea People ride in *The Voyage of the Dawn Treader*?

17. In *The Horse and his Boy*, who was made Grand Vizier: Ahoshta, Rabadash or Arsheesh?

18. What was the name of the hall full of statues of people in the palace of Charn?

19. In *The Voyage of the Dawn Treader*, who was the first to see a dragon?

20. As the *Dawn Treader* tried to get away from the island where dreams come true, what bird circled the mast?

21. After Lucy entered Narnia through the wardrobe, she walked towards light – but what was the source of the light?

22. When Aravis fled her family's home, whose armour did she wear: her father's, her stepfather's, or her brother's?

23. When Digory picked the apple of life, what colour was the bird that he encountered?

24. In *Prince Caspian*, which creature has a traditional right to act as marshals in combat: bears, badgers, centaurs or fauns?

25. In *The Lion, the Witch and the Wardrobe*, Aslan tells the dwarf that Queen Jadis must leave her wand at what tree?

26. Shasta is mistaken for a Prince of Archenland – what is his name?

27. In *The Last Battle*, what name did Rishda and the ape give to their god, a mixture of Aslan and Tash?

28. In *The Last Battle*, can you name either of the people who were going to lend Eustace and Jill the rings with which they entered Narnia?

29. Who teases Lucy cruelly for her claims that she has found a land through the wardrobe?

30. In *The Last Battle*, which creature was the first to see that the land through the doorway was a new, more colourful, Narnia: the donkey, the eagle, the unicorn or the ape?

31. Who was the shortest, fattest man that the young Prince Caspian had ever seen?

32. The bottle that Lucy was given by Father Christmas contained a cordial made from what flower: sacred sunflowers, heavenly rest rose, fire flowers or health-giving hyacinths?

33. Who is Prince Rabadash's father: King Peter, the Tisroc or King Lune?

34. In *Prince Caspian*, which child was heading off to boarding school for the very first time?

35. In *The Voyage of the Dawn Treader*, after Caspian and the others left Dragon Island, what was the name of the giant creature they saw at sea?

36. In *Prince Caspian*, Peter, Lucy, Susan and Edmund rescue a dwarf from the two soldiers in a boat. What is the dwarf's name?

37. What creature stays with Shasta on his first night near the Tombs of the Ancient Kings?

38. In *Prince Caspian*, the Seven Brothers of Shuddering Wood all did what job?

39. What is Anvard, in Archenland: a king, a castle or a village?

40. In *The Magician's Nephew*, which child has an aunt called Letitia?

41. In *Prince Caspian*, what are we told is the name of Peter's sword: Wolf's Bane, Aslan's Avenger, Rhindon, or Scarfell?

42. In *The Last Battle*, Shift says that all bulls and horses of Narnia are to be sent to work in which land?

43. In *The Magician's Nephew*, whose mother was very ill?

44. In *The Lion, the Witch and the Wardrobe*, the Witch threatens to kill two characters if either of them mention Aslan's name again. Can you remember either of them?

45. In *Prince Caspian*, which two of the following help deliver the challenge for combat to Miraz: Wimbleweather the giant, Trufflehunter, Trumpkin or Glenstorm?

46. Which one of the following was not a subject Prince Caspian had to study with his tutor: logic, rhetoric, alchemy, or versification?

47. In *The Horse and his Boy*, Shasta raids gardens on his first night out of Tashbaan. Can you name any one of the four fruits he managed to collect to eat?

48. What food was Edmund brought when he asked the Queen for Turkish delight: stale bread, chocolate cake, Turkish delight, or sticky marmalade roll?

49. What was the first creature Eustace killed in *The Last Battle*: an evil dwarf, a Calormen soldier or a giant serpent?

50. Can you name the seven friends of Narnia?

1. In *Prince Caspian*, Nikabrik suggests falling in league with which character from a previous book?

2. What are we told in *The Voyage of the Dawn Treader* is Eustace Scrubb's middle name: Clive, Claude, or Clarence?

3. Which two of the following creatures emerged from the earth in Narnia and used trees to sharpen their claws: panthers, eagles, leopards, moles, or otters?

4. In *The Last Battle*, what was the name of the Calormen captain who was in league with the ape and Ginger: Rishda, Tarkor or Garvan?

5. In *The Magician's Nephew*, which two people followed Digory on foot to meet Aslan?

6. Which character in *The Lion, the Witch and The Wardrobe* had a rocking chair: Mrs Beaver, Lucy, Glimfeather, or Reepicheep?

7. In *The Last Battle*, the doorway to the old Narnia was locked forever with a key of what colour?

8. In *The Silver Chair*, which schoolmate of Jill's arrived in Narnia shortly before her?

9. What two colours were the rings found on the tray in Uncle Andrew's study?

10. Was Bree: a little pony, a young mare, or a great war-horse?

11. When Caspian became King of Narnia, who did he make Lord Chancellor?

12. Who got cut in the mouth trying to grab Jadis's foot?

13. Before Shasta rode a horse, what was the only animal he had ever ridden?

14. In *Prince Caspian*, the children explored the ruins of Cair Paravel with a device that Edmund had received for his birthday. What was it?

15. In *The Horse and his Boy*, when Anradin barters with Arsheesh, what talking creature surprises Shasta: a badger, a fox, a horse or a donkey?

16. In *The Horse and his Boy*, who became known after his death as 'the Ridiculous'?

17. In *Prince Caspian*, what was the name of the schoolgirl from Beruna who joined Aslan's army: Brenda, Gwendolen, Emily or Hermione?

18. Jadis threatened Uncle Andrew with a spell which would make part of his body feel like blocks of ice when he lay down in bed. Which part of his body was this?

19. In *The Silver Chair*, who wore a pointed hat with an extremely wide brim: Puddleglum, Rilian or Glimfeather?

20. What was Aravis's weapon: a rapier, a broadsword, or a scimitar?

21. In *The Last Battle*, an eagle saw a Calormen banner flying over which castle in Narnia?

22. In which book would you find a dwarf called Griffle?

23. In *Prince Caspian*, Aslan led the children and Trumpkin to which landmark?

24. In *The Silver Chair*, who is most scared of dark, underground places: Jill, Eustace or Puddleglum?

25. Who entered the wardrobe for the first time and closed the door shut?

26. At what castle were Lucy, Edmund, Peter and Susan crowned kings and queens?

27. What does Eustace call Jill throughout most of *The Silver Chair*: Jilly, J or Pole?

28. In *The Magician's Nephew*, from where did Polly access the tunnel in the attic: from her mother's bedroom, from the box room, or from the larder?

29. In *The Last Battle*, who did Tirian drag with him into the stable where the god, Tash, was present?

30. In *The Magician's Nephew*, who touched noses with animals to give them the power of speech?

31. What was the name of the first talking horse Bree and Shasta encountered?

32. In *The Silver Chair*, which king did Jill and Eustace see dead at Cair Paravel?

33. Queen Prunaprismia was Prince Caspian's aunt: true or false?

34. In *The Magician's Nephew*, whose wife did Aslan fetch from another world to become Queen of Narnia?

35. Near the start of *The Last Battle*, Jewel killed a Calormen tree-cutter with what part of his body?

36. In *The Voyage of the Dawn Treader*, Caspian and the others saw a pool which turned everything into gold. On which island was this: Dragon Island, Arva Island, or Deathwater Island?

37. In *The Silver Chair*, were the parliament of owls loyal to King Caspian or against him?

38. In *The Lion, the Witch and the Wardrobe*, who did Rumblebuffin pick up by mistake, when he was after a handkerchief?

39. In *The Silver Chair*, what do the lady in green and the black knight say about the giants at Harfang: they are more rude and dangerous than those on Ettinsmoor, or they are less rude and dangerous than those on Ettinsmoor?

40. How many of the characters on the *Dawn Treader* stayed and watched over the three sleeping Lords at night?

41. Had Eustace been in Narnia before his visit in *The Silver Chair*?

42. Mr Tumnus, the faun, has the legs of what animal?

43. In *The Lion, the Witch and the Wardrobe*, is it the two boys or the two girls who warn the others about a group of sightseers walking round the Professor's house?

44. In *The Last Battle*, how many sandwiches did Eustace give to King Tirian to eat?

45. Who got a black eye from Jadis: a policeman, a jeweller, a butcher, or a judge?

46. Who grows bigger every year the children grow older?

47. In *The Lion, the Witch and the Wardrobe*, which one of the following was not a maid in the Professor's house: Margaret, Betty or Janet?

48. What item of clothing from the Professor's house did each of the children take to wear in Narnia?

49. What sort of creature had a short body, very long arms and legs, and had webbed hands like a frog?

50. What creature lay between Edmund and the entrance into the house to meet the White Witch?

QUIZ 10

1. In *Prince Caspian*, who did the Hag attack in Aslan's How: Prince Caspian, the Wer-Wolf or Doctor Cornelius?

2. In *The Last Battle*, which boy from a previous book arrived at King Tirian's aid in Lantern Waste?

3. In *Prince Caspian*, which of the children had dry matches to start a camp fire?

4. Jadis wore a piece of jewellery around her neck, stolen from a London jeweller's. What was it?

5. What did Digory do with the core of the apple of life: he threw it away, he fed it to a horse, he buried it in the garden, or he threw it in the fire?

6. In *Prince Caspian*, who did Lucy first revive with drops from the bottle given her by Aslan?

7. When Caspian discovered Dragon Island in *The Voyage of the Dawn Treader*, what year of his reign was he in: his first, his second, his third, or his fourth year?

8. In *The Horse and his Boy*, who was Aravis promised in marriage to: Ardeeb, Ahoshta or Azrooh?

9. Can you name any two of the three characters who received gifts of swords, mail shirts and helmets from the Seven Brothers of Shuddering Wood?

10. In *The Horse and his Boy*, which Queen of Narnia was Prince Rabadash possibly going to marry?

11. What type of creature attacked Prince Caspian in Aslan's How and bit him?

12. In *The Last Battle*, what was the name of the unicorn that was a close friend of the last of the Kings of Narnia?

13. In *The Magician's Nephew*, what object did Polly Plummer touch to make her vanish from Mr Ketterley's house?

14. What was the name of the Governor of the Lone Islands?

15. What was the biggest creature that Aslan breathed life back into at the Witch's house: a hippo, a giant, or a rhino?

16. What character in *The Horse and his Boy* had the full name Breehy-hinny-brinny-hoohy-hah?

17. In *The Magician's Nephew*, who was the tallest and most beautiful of the statues that Polly and Digory encountered in the palace?

18. In *The Last Battle*, according to a dryad, talking trees are being chopped down in what part of Narnia?

19. What did Bree the horse tell Shasta to do with the spurs: throw them away, wear them, or pack them so that they could be sold?

20. Which one of the following did Mrs Beaver not pack when she fled her home: a packet of tea, six clean handkerchiefs, a spare dress, or a ham?

21. Who led the horses to the Tombs outside Tashbaan: Lasaraleen's groom, Prince Rabadash's butler, or the Grand Vizier's stableboy?

22. At the start of *The Last Battle*, were Narnia and Calormen at peace or at war with each other?

23. In *Prince Caspian*, how long has passed in our world since the four children last visited Narnia: a week, a month, a year or 10 years?

24. Who was the first of the four brothers and sisters to enter Narnia through the wardrobe?

25. According to Mr Beaver, winter will end when who bares their teeth?

26. Who did Digory think was the most beautiful woman he had ever seen?

27. Who fought against Jadis in the last great battle on Charn: her sister, her mother, Aslan, or the Prince of Auchenflower?

28. Aravir is the morning star of Narnia: true or false?

29. In *Prince Caspian*, what kind of creature is Camillio: a hare, a squirrel, an otter or a badger?

30. In *Prince Caspian*, which of the following is not a feature of the Rush river gorge: silver cascades, waterfalls, amber-coloured pools, or dozens of reed beds?

31. Is Mr Tumnus's home: a straw cottage, a beavers' dam, a cave, or a log cabin?

32. In *The Lion, the Witch and the Wardrobe*, Edmund gives away the fact that he has visited Narnia before by saying that the four children should head to where?

33. Did Eustace speak to King Caspian before the King set sail for the Seven Isles?

34. In *The Lion, the Witch and the Wardrobe*, what did Aslan tell Peter always to do with his sword after battle?

35. In *The Voyage of the Dawn Treader*, who was Prince Caspian's captain on the ship?

36. The box of magic dust that Uncle Andrew used came from where: Ancient Egypt, Atlantis, China or India?

37. In *The Lion, the Witch and the Wardrobe*, which two creatures carried Aslan's crown and his standard: centaurs, leopards, fauns, or elephants?

38. In *The Horse and his Boy*, whose nickname became Thunder-Fist: Cor, Corin, Aravis, or Rabadash?

39. In *The Voyage of the Dawn Treader*, the girl who served at Aslan's Table was Aravis's sister: true or false?

40. In *Prince Caspian*, after the children ate the sandwiches packed by their mother, what was the next food they ate?

41. In *Prince Caspian*, Peter, Edmund and Trumpkin overhear a heated argument in the mound at Aslan's How which includes a badger. What was his name?

42. In *The Voyage of the Dawn Treader*, who met Lucy as she was reading the Magician's spellbook?

43. In *The Magician's Nephew*, what object normally seen on streets started to grow out of the soil?

44. Which dwarf volunteered to be a messenger for Prince Caspian?

45. Which woodland creature was chosen to be one of Prince Caspian's two messengers to get help?

46. What was the first statue that Aslan breathed back into life in the courtyard of the Witch's home?

47. What are the names of the two brothers in *The Lion, the Witch and the Wardrobe*?

48. Which one of these was not a faun who danced in front of Prince Caspian: Nausus, Tumnus, Voltinus, or Mentius?

49. In *The Magician's Nephew*, Aslan wants a fruit from what sort of tree, in order to plant a special tree to protect Narnia?

50. In *The Silver Chair*, can you name two of the three dishes beginning with the letter, M, that were to be served at the giants' Autumn Feast?

QUIZ 11

1. In *The Lion, the Witch and the Wardrobe*, in the room hung with green, what musical instrument did Lucy, Peter, Susan and Edmund spot?

2. At the end of *The Voyage of the Dawn Treader*, who did the lamb turn into?

3. In *Prince Caspian*, how many marshals were appointed at the combat between Miraz and Peter: one, three, or six?

4. In *The Last Battle*, which girl from a previous book arrived at King Tirian's aid in Lantern Waste?

5. In *The Magician's Nephew*, what was the first name of the Cabby's wife: Ivy, Lily, or Nellie?

6. Who had a bag of nine toffees which provided vital food on a journey in *The Magician's Nephew*?

7. In *Prince Caspian*, who spotted the arrival of a man at the Dancing Lawn: Camillo, Nikabrik, Peter or Susan?

8. Shift said that Puzzle might be mistaken for someone in his new coat – who?

9. In *The Lion, the Witch and the Wardrobe*, who was seeking out their brothers and sisters in a game of hide and seek?

10. In *Prince Caspian*, when the four children suddenly appeared in Narnia, how many packs of sandwiches did they have to share?

11. Who killed Maugrim, Captain of the Queen's secret police?

12. Who was the first character that Edmund met in Narnia: Lucy, the White Witch, or Mr Beaver?

13. How many lords did Miraz persuade to sail away from Narnia to search for new lands past the Eastern Ocean: three, five, seven or nine?

14. In *The Last Battle*, who was tied to an ash tree, for calling another character a liar?

15. In *Prince Caspian*, whose great-great grandfather built the castle in which Miraz lives and rules Narnia?

16. Shasta and Aravis headed away from the Tombs in which compass direction?

17. At the end of *The Last Battle*, what fell from the sky and became people with long hair?

18. In *The Silver Chair*, what sort of creature lived in the underground land of Bism: sloths, harpies, gnomes or witches?

19. On Prince Caspian's first day with Trufflehunter and the two dwarfs, who was the giant centaur he met?

20. In *Prince Caspian*, Reepicheep the mouse was a marshal in the combat between Peter and Miraz: true or false?

21. In *Prince Caspian*, after the fight inside Aslan's How, who did Peter hug and kiss: Edmund, Susan, Trufflehunter or Trumpkin?

22. Who helped Shasta escape from the house in Tashbaan in which Queen Susan and King Edmund were staying?

23. In *The Silver Chair*, Rilian and Lord Drinian saw a beautiful woman near the fountain where Rilian's mother died. What colour was her clothing?

24. When the elephant turned Uncle Andrew upside down, how many coins fell out of his pockets: three, six, 12, or 15?

25. In *The Voyage of the Dawn Treader*, what was different about the sea water in the utter east?

26. What did Shasta's real name turn out to be?

27. What was the name of the housemaid at the Ketterleys' home: Sarah, Violet, Letty, or Lily?

28. In *The Last Battle*, who was scolded by King Tirian for not cleaning his sword after combat?

29. In *The Last Battle*, King Tirian gave Eustace what sort of sword: short and pointed, broad and flat, or curved and sharp?

30. In *The Voyage of the Dawn Treader*, which one of the following was not a part of the meal that Coriakin offered Lucy: omelette, cold lamb, game pie, strawberry ice?

31. In *The Silver Chair*, after Eustace, Jill and Puddleglum cross the arched bridge, which castle do they reach?

32. In *The Last Battle*, what does King Tirian wear on a silver chain inside his clothes?

33. In *The Silver Chair*, the first giant Jill, Eustace and Puddleglum met at Harfang had what colour hair?

34. In *The Silver Chair*, the knight who rode alongside the lady in green had a horse and armour of what colour?

35. In *Prince Caspian*, which child delivered Peter's challenge for combat to Miraz?

36. In *The Last Battle*, what were the first Narnian creatures that Tirian showed the false Aslan: badgers, fauns or dwarfs?

37. When Lucy first entered Narnia, what did she find underfoot: twigs, cobbles, water, or snow?

38. In *The Silver Chair*, which giant at Harfang had a double chin and her face covered in powder?

39. In *The Horse and his Boy*, what creature was Rabadash turned into?

40. In *Prince Caspian*, the four children give Trumpkin equipment including a helmet. What type of precious stone was set into it?

41. In *Prince Caspian*, the two soldiers were trying to drown what sort of creature: a rabbit, a faun, a lion or a dwarf?

42. In *The Voyage of the Dawn Treader*, who turned into a dragon whilst they were asleep?

43. In *The Silver Chair*, who was the first person to ask Jill to do something in the name of Aslan: Eustace, King Peter, or the missing prince?

44. In *The Voyage of the Dawn Treader*, who captured Caspian and the others on Felimath: slave traders, Calormen soldiers, or Archenland bandits?

45. What item did Lucy give Mr Tumnus: a handkerchief, a ring, a coin or a thimble?

46. In *Prince Caspian*, who wrote down Peter's challenge for combat with Miraz: Susan, Doctor Cornelius, or Trufflehunter?

47. Which one of the following creatures were not present at the Stone Table when Aslan arrived to be sacrificed: Sprites, centaurs, Orknies or Wooses?

48. What pair of creatures chased Bree and Shasta the night they met Hwin and Aravis?

49. In *Prince Caspian*, what was the name of the dwarf whom Aslan pounced onto and picked up playfully in his mouth?

50. In *The Silver Chair*, who sprinkled green powder onto the fire to weave an enchantment in Underland?

QUIZ 12

1. In *The Silver Chair*, at the first dinner Eustace and Jill have in Narnia, they hear a blind poet tell the tale of one of the other Narnia books. Which one?

2. Who climbed a tree at the Stone Table to evade an attack by a wolf?

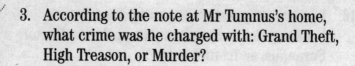

3. According to the note at Mr Tumnus's home, what crime was he charged with: Grand Theft, High Treason, or Murder?

4. In *The Voyage of the Dawn Treader*, what nickname did Pug give Edmund: fatty, sulky, or know-it-all?

5. Which character's house had hams and strings of onions hanging from the roof?

6. In *The Horse and his Boy*, which castle in Narnia does Prince Rabadash intend to visit first with his army?

7. In *The Silver Chair*, what letter in the words 'Under Me' had Jill and Eustace explored as a snowy trench when on their way to Harfang?

8. In *The Magician's Nephew*, who knew the secret of the Deplorable Word?

9. Who did Mr Tumnus have a picture of, over his mantelpiece: Queen Jadis, Aslan, his father or the Elf Lord?

10. Doctor Cornelius and Prince Caspian watched which two of the following planets pass close by each other: Tarva, Famor, Heracles, Alambil or Senos?

11. Who was very tempted to utter a spell to make her the most beautiful woman in the world: Susan, Lucy or Aravis?

12. Miraz was a ruler of Narnia: true or false?

13. In *The Last Battle*, who was the only dwarf heading for the mines who still believed in Aslan and followed Tirian and the others to the tower?

14. In *The Voyage of the Dawn Treader*, who caught Eustace taking an unfair share of the drinking water at night?

15. What do the letters C and S stand for, in CS Lewis?

16. When Shasta was at the Tombs of the Ancient Kings, which two horses did he see coming towards him?

17. In *Prince Caspian*, what sort of animal was Clodsey Shovel?

18. In *The Magician's Nephew*, who locked the door to their study after discovering two children in the room?

19. After Digory had rung the bell in the Palace of Charn, how many people awoke: one, three or five?

20. Who had owned the box of magic dust before Uncle Andrew took it?

21. What sort of bird made the first ever joke in Narnia: a parrot, a jackdaw, a woodpecker or a cuckoo?

22. When Edmund first met the Queen, how many drops from her magic bottle gave him a warm drink served in a jewelled cup?

23. In *The Lion, the Witch and the Wardrobe*, what sort of creature was Maugrim?

24. In *The Silver Chair*, Aslan gives Jill signs to help her on her quest – but how many: two, three, four, or six?

25. After the battle with Miraz's forces, who was Prince Caspian reunited with: his nurse, his father, or his pet cat?

26. What item did Mr Beaver show the children to prove that he knew Mr Tumnus?

27. By the time Jill and Eustace meet a character found in many Narnia books, he is deaf and uses a silver ear trumpet. Who is he?

28. What relation were Mr and Miss Ketterley?

29. In *The Lion, the Witch and the Wardrobe*, who guides the children to their first meeting with Aslan?

30. In *The Voyage of the Dawn Treader*, after Lucy, Edmund and Eustace have said goodbye to Reepicheep, what creature invites them to breakfast?

31. Who was the first on the *Dawn Treader* to spot the underwater castle of the Sea People?

32. In *The Horse and his Boy*, how did Susan and Edmund arrive at Tashbaan: on horseback, by foot, in a ship or by a flying carpet?

33. Which one of the following was called to Aslan's first council in Narnia: the Bull-Elephant, the Naiad daughters, or the Chief Eagle?

34. At the end of *The Voyage of the Dawn Treader*, which two children does Aslan say will not come back to Narnia again?

35. In *Prince Caspian*, we are told that when Miraz first took over Narnia, he gave himself what title: King Miraz, Emperor of the Lost Lands, Lord Protector, or Earl of Erindina?

36. Who takes a yellow ring to try to follow and rescue Polly?

37.   Whose home looked like a giant beehive to Lucy, Peter, Susan and Edmund?

38.   A lion forced Shasta to join with Aravis and also drove the jackals away. What was his name?

39.   In *The Lion, the Witch and the Wardrobe*, Lucy, Peter and Susan were in an old beavers' hiding place when they heard what sort of sound: howling wolves, jingling bells, or a lion's roar?

40.   What did Aravis do to escape from her family home: drug a maid, fight her brother, or imprison her mother?

41.   In *The Last Battle*, what did Tirian and Jewel fill the Calormen sentry's mouth with at Stable Hill, so that he couldn't make a sound?

42.   Where did Peter, Susan, Edmund and Lucy hide to avoid Mrs Macready and the sightseers?

43.   In *The Last Battle*, what is the name of the giant at Cair Paravel: Hornfoot, Clubfoot or Stonefoot?

44.   Where does Shift say that digging animals like moles are to be sent to work?

45.   In *The Silver Chair*, a green serpent killed which royal family member of Narnia?

46. Aslan knights Peter at the Stone Table. What title does he give him?

47. In *Prince Caspian*, what type of creature are the three Hardbiters: a type of dog, a type of wolf, or a type of badger?

48. Which one of the following did Jadis not ask Uncle Andrew to get as transport for her: a flying carpet, a steam train, or a well-trained dragon?

49. Jill, Eustace and Puddleglum found the Black Knight bound to a chair of what colour?

50. How many soldiers did Aravis and Shasta have to walk past at Tashbaan city gates?

QUIZ 13

1. Who drank two glasses of wine after his first encounter with Jadis: Miss Ketterley, Mr Beaver, or Uncle Andrew?

2. In *The Horse and his Boy*, who escaped Tashbaan by pretending to hold a great feast on their ship and then sailing off: Narnians, Shasta and Aravis, or Aslan?

3. In *The Magician's Nephew*, which girl asked to accompany Digory on his quest?

4. In *The Last Battle*, when Eustace arrived in Narnia, what sort of bag was he carrying with him?

5. What is the name of the evil queen who wakes up in the world of Charn?

6. Did elves, pixies or satyrs come out of the wood along with gods and goddesses when Aslan called them?

7. In *The Voyage of the Dawn Treader*, who was spotted by Caspian wearing Lord Octesian's arm-ring: a dragon, a pirate, Lucy, or Reepicheep?

8. What creature dug jewels for the crowns for the first King and Queen of Narnia: moles, beavers, earthworms, or otters?

9. In *The Last Battle*, how many arms did Tash appear to have?

10. In *The Silver Chair*, what was the name of the enormous figure, much larger than a giant, that Jill and the others saw in Underland?

11. What animal attacked Hwin after they had just arrived in Archenland?

12. Shift sewed the lion skin for whom to wear as a coat?

13. In *The Lion, the Witch and the Wardrobe*, at what place did the children first see an Incubus?

14. Who felt sick after eating sweets from the Queen of Narnia?

15. In *Prince Caspian*, when the travellers are voting whether they go up or down the gorge, who is the only character to side with Lucy?

16. What type of creature collected thistles to try to feed Uncle Andrew with?

17. In *Prince Caspian*, which dwarf brought two strangers to the council meeting in the mound at Aslan's How?

18. What type of dwarf was Trumpkin: a red dwarf, a black dwarf, or a half-dwarf?

19. In *The Last Battle*, which one of the following was not one of the seven who met Tirian in the stable: Peter, Edmund, Susan, or Lucy?

20. In *The Lion, the Witch and the Wardrobe*, all the stools in the Beavers' house had how many legs: three, four or five?

21. Mr Beaver went fishing for dinner for himself, his wife and the four children. What type of fish did he catch?

22. Who ate a silver apple: Digory, Aslan, the Witch, or Polly?

23. Doctor Cornelius told Prince Caspian of three especially sacred places in Narnia. Can you name one of them?

24. Who is asked by Aslan to get a seed from a special place, so that Aslan can plant a tree which will protect Narnia?

25. In *The Voyage of the Dawn Treader*, after Eustace had stopped being a dragon, who was the first to meet him?

26. Who did Jill Pole meet at the start of *The Silver Chair*?

27. Who felt terrible that they had not helped rescue Aravis and Hwin from the lion?

28. In *The Magician's Nephew*, what new name does Aslan give the horse, Strawberry?

29. In *The Horse and his Boy*, who has 19 sons: the Tisroc, King Lune, or Aravis's father?

30. In *The Lion, the Witch and the Wardrobe*, how many wolves did the Witch send to the Beavers' house?

31. Prince Caspian meets a talkative squirrel who offers him a nut. What is the squirrel's name?

32. What was the name of the place where Prince Caspian and the talking animals and other Old Narnia creatures held their first council?

33. In *The Last Battle*, what was the name of the donkey who was Shift's friend?

34. In *Prince Caspian*, the children rescue a dwarf. Is he: a messenger, a traitor, a thief, or a doctor?

35. After Prince Caspian met the Seven Brothers of Shuddering Wood, how many black dwarfs did he meet?

36. In *The Magician's Nephew*, what sort of sweet did Digory plant in Narnia which resulted the next day in a tree?

37. In *The Lion, the Witch and the Wardrobe*, where are the children supposed to meet Aslan: at the lamp post, at the Stone Table, at Cair Paravel, or at Lantern Waste?

38. Where was a pavilion with ivory poles and yellow silk sides: at the Lantern Waste, at the Stone Table or at Cair Paravel?

39. By what other name was Caspian the First known?

40. What was the name of Prince Caspian's ship: the *Splendour Hyaline*, the *Dawn Treader*, the *Saucy Sue*, or the *Valiant Voyager*?

41. Was a theorbo: a type of sprite, a musical instrument, a weapon or an ancient law?

42. In *The Horse and his Boy*, who was the only daughter of Kidrash Tarkaan: Aravis, Cor, or Peradin?

43. Was Miss Prizzle a teacher, a priestess or the ruler of Beruna?

44. In *The Silver Chair*, who did the serpent try to kill by coiling round him?

45. Who rode with Prince Rilian on the Prince's horse?

46. In *The Silver Chair*, who is the old, frail king who sets sail from Cair Paravel?

47. Which creature in *The Last Battle* repeatedly says that he is not very clever?

48. In *The Silver Chair*, the Earthmen of Underland all carry what sort of weapon?

49. In *The Silver Chair*, Aslan tells Jill that she and Eustace must journey out of Narnia in which compass direction?

50. When Lucy had tea with Mr Tumnus, which one of the following was not on the menu: sardines, boiled egg, currant buns, or toast with honey?

QUIZ 14

1. Was the island where the great feast at Aslan's Table was set known as: The Full Circle, World's End, or The Witch's Retreat?

2. In *Prince Caspian*, which of the hungry children on the island suggested they search for gull's eggs?

3. In *The Last Battle*, was Slinky the fox fighting for or against Tirian, Eustace and Jill?

4. Which boat was drawn onto land and repaired and refitted at Narrowhaven?

5. In *The Silver Chair*, who carried Puddleglum's second-best bow for protection: Puddleglum, Eustace, or Jill?

6. Which sort of Narnian creature has two breakfasts every morning – one for its horse stomach and one for its man stomach?

7. What was the name of the first ever Queen of Narnia?

8. Which character is first seen by Lucy, Edmund, Susan and Peter sitting at her sewing machine?

9. Which character grows up to become the famous Professor Kirke?

10. What type of creature told the Witch that Father Christmas had visited: a dog-fox, a wolf, or a beaver?

11. Who urged the crew of the *Dawn Treader* to head into the darkness?

12. What was the name of Prince Caspian's tutor?

13. In *The Silver Chair*, who is told by Aslan to seek out the missing Prince of Narnia?

14. What item did Aslan ask Eustace to drive into his paw to draw blood?

15. In *Prince Caspian*, when Peter issues a combat challenge to Miraz, which of the following is not one of his titles: Lord of Cair Paravel, Emperor of the Lone Islands, or Chief of Narnia's Realms?

16. What is the name of the god of the land of Calormen?

17. After the *Dawn Treader* visited Dragon Island, which island did it visit next?

18. Who arrived near the Ketterleys' house driving a hansom cab by standing on its roof?

19. In *Prince Caspian*, which one of the children would Trumpkin travel with if the group of children split up?

20. Edmund ate Turkish delight from a box tied with what: a green ribbon, a piece of white rope, or black iron wire?

21. In *The Silver Chair*, what did the Warder of the Marches of Underland call Jill, Eustace and Puddleglum: Overworld creatures, Aboveland creatures, or Skyfell creatures?

22. What colour robe was the Magician wearing in *The Voyage of the Dawn Treader*?

23. Who is tied to a silver chair every night in Underland: the Black Knight, the Queen of the Giants, the Queen of Underland, or Glimfeather?

24. In *The Last Battle*, who does King Tirian order to run to Cair Paravel to bring soldiers to attack forces in Lantern Waste?

25. Doctor Cornelius tells Caspian about Old Narnia in what part of Miraz's castle: the Eastern Battlements, the ballroom, the stables, or the Great Central Tower?

26. What was the name of the first marsh-wiggle Jill and Eustace met?

27. In *The Last Battle*, after the old Narnia disappears, who did Eustace, Tirian and the others find sitting underneath a chestnut tree: Rishda, Ahoshta, or Emeth the Calormen soldier?

28. Which two children go through a door in the stone wall of their school grounds to enter another world?

29. In *The Magician's Nephew*, which two characters fled as Aslan approached, after he had been hit with an iron bar?

30. What is the name of the badger who helped revive Prince Caspian with a drink?

31. In *The Last Battle*, whose last words were 'I don't understand': the bear, the boar or the satyr?

32. What was Eustace's father called: Herbert, Hubert, or Harold?

33. Who grabbed Polly by her hair and insisted that they go back to Polly and Digory's world?

34. Which child spitefully swung Reepicheep round by his tail?

35. In *The Magician's Nephew*, we are told that the last great battle in Charn went on for how many days: three, 15, 20 or 50?

36. What was Eustace's mother's name: Alice, Alberta, or Althea?

37. Whose roar summoned up nymphs, Bacchus and dozens of other creatures?

38. In *The Last Battle*, can you name any of the foods that the animals fed King Tirian when he was tied up?

39. Which one of the following is not a member of King Lune's forces: Shar, Tran, Feldar, or Colin?

40.   What was the name of the last King of Narnia?

41.   In *Prince Caspian*, Nikabrik claims that the
creatures who are first to lose out when rations
are short are what: dwarfs, squirrels, mice, or
centaurs?

42.   In *The Magician's Nephew*, who starts to plot a
way of making a fortune through 'growing' steel
battleships, trains and other things in Narnia?

43.   Eustace and his family lived in which English
town: Oxford, Bristol, Cambridge, or Exeter?

44.   In *The Last Battle*, as Narnia's time ends, two
types of creature tear up the remains of Narnia's
forests. Can you name either of them?

45.   After Father Christmas has visited, what sort
of sandwiches does Mrs Beaver make?

46.   In *The Silver Chair*, which one of the following
was not part of the meal that Jill enjoyed on her
first night in Harfang: cock-a-leekie soup, roast
chestnuts, roast pheasant, or roast turkey?

47.   In which book was Glasswater Creek first
mentioned: *The Silver Chair*, *The Last Battle*,
or *Prince Caspian*?

48. Who became known as 'the Just', when they were a ruler of Narnia: Lucy, Edmund or Peter?

49. In *The Magician's Nephew*, which human found himself caged, and had worms and a honeycomb thrown at him?

50. How many crescents did Shasta find in Bree's saddlebags: 20, 40, 60 or 100?

QUIZ 15

1. Which creature did the digging for the orchard to be planted at Cair Paravel?

2. Who out of these four children is second to reach Narnia: Edmund, Lucy, Peter or Susan?

3. In *The Silver Chair*, what creature appears just as Eustace falls over the cliff?

4. In *The Last Battle*, which group of creatures refuses to join sides in the battle between Tirian's forces and Rishda's?

5. Jadis threatened Uncle Andrew with a spell which would make anything he sat down on feel like what red-hot metal?

6. In *Prince Caspian*, what sort of building do the four children find on the island: a troll's hut, a church, a castle or a cottage?

7. What type of creature is the first talking animal that Prince Caspian ever encounters?

8. In *The Voyage of the Dawn Treader*, on the island the crew visit after Dragon Island, who sat on an old rusted sword?

9. In *The Last Battle*, what was the name, beginning with the letter, F, of the eagle which brought terrible news to King Tirian?

10. In *The Voyage of the Dawn Treader*, who taught the Duffers how to walk on water: Aslan, Reepicheep or Eustace?

11. In *The Last Battle*, whose closest friend was a unicorn?

12. In *The Lion, the Witch and the Wardrobe*, how did the White Witch arrive in front of Edmund: on foot, carried by dwarfs or on a sledge?

13. Which one of the following was not a city that Queen Jadis said she had destroyed: Charn, Manatu, Felinda or Sorlois?

14. Rhindon was a wizard who lived in Trufflehunter's Cave: true or false?

15. At the end of *The Last Battle*, who did Emeth meet between two rocks: Peter, Eustace, King Tirian, or Aslan?

16. Which one of the children sneaks out of Mr and Mrs Beaver's house without the others?

17. In *The Last Battle*, how many towers were there guarding Lantern Waste?

18. Is Calormen a land: to the north of Narnia, the west of Narnia, or the south of Narnia?

19. Who was the first of the *Dawn Treader's* crew to eat from Aslan's Table: Reepicheep, Eustace, Edmund or Lucy?

20. The fat dwarf who worked for the White Witch wore polar-bear fur. What colour was his hood?

21. In *The Silver Chair*, as the travellers saw Harfang for the first time, what bird did Puddleglum shoot with his bow and arrow?

22. What is the name of the smaller river which joins the Great River at Beruna?

23. In *The Lion, the Witch and the Wardrobe*, when the Queen wanted to hunt down Lucy, Peter and Susan, what vehicle did she order fitted with harnesses without bells?

24. In *The Last Battle*, did King Tirian send for 10 dwarf archers or 10 centaur warriors to head for Lantern Waste?

25. In *Prince Caspian*, did the children arrive in Narnia: in a mountain range, on an island, or in a desert?

26. On the first day of Shasta's escape with Bree, which of the following was not part of his breakfast: blue cheese, dried figs, or a meat pasty?

27. In *Prince Caspian*, is Doctor Cornelius: a dwarf, a half-dwarf or a jinn?

28. What name did Caspian first give Deathwater Island?

29. Who was the youngest of the brothers in *The Lion, the Witch and the Wardrobe*?

30. In *Prince Caspian*, who did Edmund, Peter and Trumpkin encounter as sentries at the entrance to the mound at Aslan's How: badgers, centaurs or dwarfs?

31. What was the name of the Lord that the *Dawn Treader* picked up in the darkness?

32. How many upright stones support the Stone Table?

33. According to Mr Tumnus, where do dryads live: in trees, in rivers and streams or in deserts?

34. In *The Last Battle*, was Wraggle the satyr fighting on the side of Tirian, Eustace and Jill or against them?

35. The top half of a centaur is like a man, but what animal is their bottom half like?

36. In *The Voyage of the Dawn Treader*, over what meal did Caspian, Edmund and the others realise that Eustace had gone missing?

37. What is the name of the currency in Calormen: dowts, crescents, tashens or spirals?

38. From what county did the Ketterleys originally come: Surrey, Dorset, Somerset or Devon?

39. In *The Last Battle*, what was the name of the railway company whose train Jill and Eustace had been travelling on when they suddenly arrived in Narnia?

40. In *The Silver Chair*, what is the name of the marsh-wiggle who accompanies Eustace and Jill on their adventures?

41. Where did the children end up at the very end of *Prince Caspian*?

42. At the end of *The Horse and his Boy*, who became Queen of Archenland?

43. In *The Horse and his Boy*, which castle in Archenland did Prince Rabadash intend to seize first with his forces?

44. In *The Last Battle*, when King Tirian cries 'Home!' where should Jill and Eustace flee to: Cair Paravel, the tower in Lantern Waste, or the village of Beaversdam?

45. In *The Lion, the Witch and the Wardrobe*, how many days had passed back in the Professor's house when the four children returned from their many years as rulers of Narnia: none, one, seven or 14?

46. In *The Lion, the Witch and the Wardrobe*, what item does Aslan insist the Queen leave behind if they are to meet: her stone knife, her wand, or her spear?

47. As a young boy, who was Prince Caspian's favourite person: his uncle, his nurse, his aunt, or Sir Leonard?

48. In *The Last Battle*, who ordered King Tirian to be tied up: the White Witch, Shift or Queen of the Underland?

49. In *Prince Caspian*, which one of the children was the most grumpy at being woken up and forced to follow Lucy?

50. In *The Last Battle*, Peter, Edmund and Lucy's parents were on a train bound for where: London, Cambridge or Bristol?

QUIZ 16

1. In *Prince Caspian*, what item did Doctor Cornelius say was the most precious treasure in the whole of Narnia?

2. Which of the children received a bow and quiver full of arrows from Father Christmas?

3. Prince Caspian was on his voyage to find seven friends of whose: his father's, Peter's or Aslan's?

97

4. The tree which grew from the core of the apple of life was eventually cut down and its wood made into what item of furniture?

5. What part of Digory did the Queen grab so that she could travel back with the children to London?

6. Who did Jadis throw an iron bar at, aiming for their head?

7. Lasaraleen recognised one of the two runaways in Tashbaan – but was it Aravis or Shasta?

8. In *The Last Battle*, after heading through the doorway out of Narnia, which compass direction did Eustace, Lucy and the others head?

9. In *The Silver Chair*, when Jill and Eustace arrived in Narnia, how long had it been since Prince Rilian disappeared: more than one year, 10 years, 20 years or 100 years?

10. Which one of the following did the Queen not show Digory and Polly as they walked through the palace at Charn: the stables, the dungeons, or the torture chamber?

11. Who says that at a certain time each night he turns into a giant serpent: Aslan, the Black Knight, or Lord Darrin?

12. How many thrones are there at Cair Paravel castle?

13. Which of Prince Caspian's loyal dwarfs did not believe in Peter, Susan, Lucy and Edmund once being Kings and Queens of Narnia?

14. According to Mr Beaver, who was Queen Jadis's mother: Lilith, Eustace, or Hermione?

15. In *The Horse and his Boy*, who repeatedly kicks the Grand Vizier when they are having a secret meeting in the Tisroc's palace?

16. Who was the oldest out of Trumpkin, Nikabrik and Trufflehunter?

17. In *Prince Caspian*, was the train to take the girls coming half an hour before or after the train to take the boys?

18. In *The Last Battle*, can you name one of the three types of animal which brought King Tirian his dinner when he was tied up?

19. What was the name of the girl who rode on Hwin?

20. What is the name of the horse who can talk and runs away with Shasta?

21. In *Prince Caspian*, what did DLF come to stand for: Dear Little Friend, Deadly Lantern Field, or Dangerous Little Fiend?

22. After Uncle Andrew's adventures in Narnia, did he become: more evil, less evil or stay as evil as he had been before?

23. In *The Last Battle*, which creatures started killing the released talking horses?

24. Was Queen Lucy, King Peter or King Edmund known as 'the Valiant'?

25. In *The Last Battle*, what was the name of the most huge of the creatures that Aslan summoned?

26. Who will become King of Archenland after King Lune?

27. What word is used to describe people who came from the Land of Telmar?

28. How does Bree tell Shasta he should hold on when riding: with his hands, with his arms or with his knees?

29. Can you name either of the presents that Father Christmas gives Peter?

30. In *Prince Caspian*, can you name two of the three characters who skinned and collected meat off of the grey bear that had attacked Lucy?

31. Who asked Aunt Letty to lend him five pounds?

32. In *The Silver Chair*, what sort of water creature did the marsh-wiggle catch and cook for Jill and Eustace's breakfast?

33. What did Digory and Polly think Uncle Andrew used the attic for: to hide a mad wife, to perform experiments, or to hide weapons?

34. Which one of the following was not called to Aslan's first council in Narnia: the River-God, the He-Owl, or the Head Faun?

35. What did Aslan do to Uncle Andrew: fight him, tie him in chains, send him to sleep, or poison him?

36. In *Prince Caspian*, what colour hair did Queen Prunaprismia have?

37. In *The Last Battle*, what was the name of the creature Jill untied and escaped with from Stable Hill?

38. In *The Lion, the Witch and the Wardrobe*, which two children followed Aslan as he left the camp for the Stone Table at night-time?

39. What jewel was set in the crown of Queen Helen of Narnia?

40. Which creature grabbed the sun in his hand to create total darkness?

41. What sort of creature was spotted singing the most beautiful song when Polly and the others arrived in the new world?

42. Who jumped overboard just after the Sea People had been spotted: Drinian, Rhince, Eustace or Reepicheep?

43. What city is the home of the court of the Tisroc in *The Horse and his Boy*?

44. In *Prince Caspian*, who discovered the knight chess piece: Lucy, Susan or Peter?

45. Who did Digory spot close to him just as he picked the silver apple?

46. In *Prince Caspian*, how many steps led down from the door into the treasure chamber: 10, 16, 24 or 40?

47. What woodland creature gave Uncle Andrew nuts to eat?

48. Who kept Narnia in winter: the Black Witch, the White Witch, or the Green Witch?

49. Was it Telmarines, half-dwarfs or mer-men who killed and drove away the dwarfs and fauns of Old Narnia?

50. Who carried the train of the first King of Narnia during his coronation: dwarfs, elves, fauns or magpies?

QUIZ 17

1. What food do the Three Bulgy Bears offer Prince Caspian?

2. What is a Tarkaan: a type of fishing boat, a village in the desert, or a great lord?

3. In what chamber at Cair Paravel does a magical map of the voyage of the *Dawn Treader* hang?

4. In *The Last Battle*, where did King Tirian first meet High King Peter: Cair Paravel, Archenland, or on Stable Hill?

5. After Prince Caspian has fallen from his horse, how many creatures caught him and tended him?

6. In *The Last Battle*, had dwarfs, goblins or centaurs taught Shift how to sew?

7. After fleeing Mr and Mrs Beaver's house, who was the next person, Lucy, Peter and Susan saw?

8. In *The Magician's Nephew*, who calls London a hole, when speaking to Polly?

9. In *Prince Caspian*, who won the fencing contest between Trumpkin and one of the children?

10. Can you remember any one of the three things, according to Doctor Cornelius, that dwarfs did in the past to escape being identified?

11. In *The Silver Chair*, who does the Black Knight turn out to be?

12. Where was Mr Ketterley's study: in the basement, on the ground floor, or the top floor of the house?

13. In *The Voyage of the Dawn Treader*, who suggested the name Deathwater Island: Lucy, Edmund, Reepicheep or Rhince?

14. In *The Silver Chair*, who opened the door to Jill's room, whilst trapped in Harfang castle: the nurse, the Queen or the porter of the giants?

15. Who broke a fine porcelain vase as they climbed through the window of the room that Shasta was sleeping in?

16. In *The Last Battle*, what sort of food did King Tirian, Peter, Edmund and the others first eat together: swan, pheasant, fruit or cheese?

17. What broke Aunt Letty's fall after she was thrown by the Queen: some cushions, a mattress, Uncle Andrew, or a pile of washing?

18. Which of the children's hats did they use to carry the fish back to the island in *Prince Caspian*?

19. In *The Last Battle*, which creature turned from a talking beast to a non-talking beast by the power of the god inside the stable?

20. In *The Last Battle*, who had been kicked and was to be executed the next day before being rescued by Tirian?

21. In *The Magician's Nephew*, who rode on a horse to reach Aslan so that he could talk about his mother?

22. In *The Silver Chair*, the door from which room connected with the kitchens led directly to the outer wall of Harfang castle?

23. In *The Silver Chair*, on what bird's back did Jill leave Cair Paravel?

24. In *The Voyage of the Dawn Treader*, what is the the date of the first entry in Eustace's diary: 9th May, 15th July, 7th August or 10th September?

25. Who had saved the people of the Lone Islands from a dragon: King Gale, King Frank or King Caspian?

26. In *The Last Battle*, how old was King Tirian: 16 years of age, between 20 and 25, between 30 and 35, or over 60 years old?

27. When the Old Man sang at World's End, hundreds of what type of creature arrived?

28. In *The Last Battle*, which child did King Tirian give a bow and a quiver full of arrows to?

29. What was the name of the Queen of Underland's horse: Darkness, Thunderer or Snowflake?

30. Who put an uglifying spell on the invisible people in *The Voyage of the Dawn Treader*: Aslan, Coriakin, or the Tisroc?

31. Who turns out to be Shasta's father?

32. Who did the Queen offer the post of Prince and, later, King of Narnia: Edmund, Peter, or Mr Tumnus?

33. Where was Pattertwig sent by Prince Caspian: to Cair Paravel, Miraz's castle, or Lantern Waste?

34. Which two out of Edmund, Peter, Susan and Lucy were to stay with the Scrubbs in *The Voyage of the Dawn Treader*?

35. At the very end of *The Last Battle*, what word, beginning with the letter, S, does Aslan call all other lands away from his own?

36. In *The Last Battle*, was Farsight the eagle fighting for or against Tirian, Eustace and Jill?

37. Who dressed up like workmen to dig out the magic rings from the garden of the London house?

38. In *The Lion, the Witch and the Wardrobe*, who refused to back up Lucy's story about Narnia to the other children: Peter, Susan or Edmund?

39. Who left the Ketterleys' house in a cab along with Jadis?

40. Which creature would awake on the day that Narnia ended: Trumpkin, the White Witch, or Old Father Time?

41. According to Aslan in *The Magician's Nephew*, Archenland and Narnia are separated by what range of mountains?

42. Who reckons the White Witch will saw their horns off: Glenstorm the centaur, Mr Beaver, or Mr Tumnus?

43. Did Queen Jadis use a knife, an axe, her fingernails or her teeth to cut the harness holding the horse to the smashed hansom cab?

44. In the pool on Deathwater Island, which one of the following did Caspian and the others not see turn to gold: a spear, a helmet, some heather?

45. Which colour ring draws you to the Wood Between the Worlds?

46. Who stayed behind as the *Dawn Treader* set sail for the end of the world: Rhince, Drinian or Pittencream?

47. Who kept a diary on the voyage of the *Dawn Treader*: Eustace, Edmund or Lucy?

48. In *The Horse and his Boy*, which Lord carried the great banner of Narnia: Peridan, Thornbut, or Darrin?

49. What creature, if caught, gives you two wishes?

50. In *The Magician's Nephew*, what did the hansom cab crash into: another hansom cab, a fire hydrant, a lamp post, or a police wagon?

QUIZ 18

1. Which of the four Pevensie children had won prizes for swimming at school?

2. For every treachery in Narnia, Jadis has the right to what: a gold coin, a kill, 10 new slaves, or a new weapon?

3. Which Prince in *The Horse and his Boy* wants his father to invade Narnia?

4. Which of the four Pevensie children watched the Witch turn a family of squirrels, a dog-fox and two satyrs into stone?

5. With what weapon did the White Witch kill Aslan?

6. In *The Silver Chair*, by what time of the day was one supposed to reach Harfang before they locked all their doors: 9am, noon, 3pm, or sunset?

7. Who got a fright when they saw their face in the bearded mirror: Edmund, Eustace or Lucy?

8. Who kidnapped Shasta when he was a very young child: Lord Bar, Prince Cor, or Lord Darrin?

9. Which character from Narnia got five minutes in the world of Jill and Eustace?

10. Who owned a house which had bunks for beds: Mr Tumnus, Queen Jadis, or Mr and Mrs Beaver?

11. Who asked Polly if she had forgiven Digory for the argument and struggle in the Hall of Images at Charn?

12. What was the name of Prince Caspian's horse: Destrier, Charger, Valiant or Geldvar?

13. In *The Magician's Nephew*, whose great-grandfather killed 700 nobles in the banqueting hall?

14. When all four thrones are filled correctly at Cair Paravel, who is to lose their life?

15. How many corners does a Narnian shield have?

16. In *Prince Caspian*, which one of the children nearly lost his temper with Trumpkin after he belittled them as children and did not believe they had fought in battles?

17. Tashbaan is the capital city of which land?

18. When did Polly and Digory meet each other: in the Easter break, the Summer holidays or around Christmas time?

19. Who took off his sword as he continued alone towards the end of the world?

20. In *The Last Battle*, who does Aslan tell Emeth is his opposite?

21. What sort of creature did the dwarf say were thought to be on the island containing Cair Paravel: ghosts, giants or rats?

22. In *The Lion, the Witch and the Wardrobe*, who first mentions that Aslan may be on the move?

23. At the start of *The Silver Chair*, who was crying because she had been bullied?

24. Which of the children received a small dagger from Father Christmas?

25. In *The Silver Chair*, what musical instrument did the Queen of Underland play to make an enchantment over Jill, Eustace, Puddleglum and Rilian?

26. What little creatures helped gnaw away the ropes that tied Aslan?

27. When the four Pevensie children ate dinner with Mr and Mrs Beaver, what did they drink: ginger beer, milk, cherryade, or dandelion wine?

28. In *Prince Caspian*, Lucy rediscovered the bottle of magic medicine given to her by Father Christmas. Was it now: full, over half full, less than a quarter full, or empty?

29. In Narnia, what is the northernmost star in the sky called: the Pole Star, the Spear-Head or the Sword-Point?

30. What bottled drink did Polly drink in the attic of her house?

31. What item did Digory use to cut a strip of turf in the bank of the pool to mark it?

32. What was the name of the magician in *The Voyage of the Dawn Treader*?

33. Whose army did Shasta and Aravis see almost immediately they entered Archenland?

34. What river creature piloted a raft made of freshly-cut trees to sell to Calormen?

35. What sort of clothing did Lucy discover in the magic wardrobe?

36. Who had to pawn their watch and chain in order to buy Jadis a very expensive lunch?

37. What part of his body did Eustace the dragon use to kill animals to feed Caspian and the others?

38. In *The Last Battle*, what weapon was used to kill the talking horses?

39. When Digory, Polly and Uncle Andrew returned to London from Narnia, who was the first to have a bath?

40. What is the name of the talking mouse which befriends Prince Caspian?

41. Whose cave did Eustace sleep in after he had left the others repairing the *Dawn Treader*?

42. What flying horse were Digory and Polly reunited with in *The Last Battle*?

43. How many reindeer pulled the White Witch's sledge?

44. When Jill first arrived in Narnia, did she immediately see: a quayside, a castle, or both?

45. Who doesn't like to see women walking around with bare arms: Mr Ketterley, Aunt Letty, Digory, or Frank the Cabby?

46. What sound did Polly and Digory hear in Uncle Andrew's study: a crackling, a humming or a clanking sound?

47. In *The Silver Chair*, who was brought all sorts of toys including dolls and rocking horses in their first night at Harfang?

48. What was the name of the centaur who brought news to King Tirian about whether the sky and the stars foretell the arrival of Aslan?

49. In *The Silver Chair*, whose sword blow on the serpent had no effect: Eustace's, Rilian's or Puddleglum's?

50. In *The Last Battle*, who shot Wraggle the satyr with an arrow?

1. Who was the first to call Shift a liar: King Tirian, Jewel, or Lady Polly?

2. What were the names of the two sisters in *The Lion, the Witch and the Wardrobe*?

3. In *The Last Battle*, what title did the Calormen give Shift: Mouthpiece of Aslan, Prophet of the Stars, or Lord of all Talking Animals?

4. In *The Last Battle*, which one of the people in Tirian's dream gave his title as 'the High King'?

5. In *The Magician's Nephew*, which child had turned the space behind the cistern in the attic into a smuggler's cave?

6. In *The Lion, the Witch and the Wardrobe*, who did Edmund have a talk with before being reunited with his brother and sisters?

7. What creature did Jill manage to shoot with her bow and arrow during archery practice with King Tirian?

8. Does Aslan's How lie in the Great Woods or the Wild Lands of the North?

9. Whose mother was Mrs Kirke?

10. Which human character in *The Magician's Nephew* wore a top hat which became battered?

11. In *Prince Caspian*, which child fired an arrow at the soldiers to stop the dwarf from being drowned?

12. What was the name of the boy who lived with Arsheesh?

13. During the battle in *The Lion, the Witch and the Wardrobe*, how many ogres did Edmund fight his way past to reach the Witch?

14. Who always claimed he was smarter than Puzzle and made Puzzle do all the work?

15. Which human character in *The Magician's Nephew* wore a bowler hat?

16. Where was Mrs Lefay's special box of magic dust hidden: in her dresser, her bureau, her vegetable basket, or in her wardrobe?

17. Which girl dressed in a short cloak with a hood and shorts to leave Cair Paravel?

18. In the palace at Charn, what hung from a golden arch and could be hit with a golden hammer?

19. In *The Last Battle*, who gave themselves up as murderers to the Calormen?

20. In *The Lion, the Witch and the Wardrobe*, who left the three children and the two beavers with a giant teapot full of tea?

21. Did Polly and Digory put their green and yellow rings in their pockets, their knapsacks, or in their shoes?

22. Who started singing a harvest thanksgiving hymn after they had travelled from London into a new world?

23. The first time that Polly and Digory used the yellow rings, where did they end up: in Aslan's lair, the Wood Between the Worlds, or in Jadis's palace?

24. Which two children in *The Silver Chair* struggled on the edge of the cliff with one falling over?

25. In *The Last Battle*, what were grease and ashes mixed up by Poggin to remove: blood from chain mail, a brownish dye from skin, or poison from a wound?

26. On the four Pevensie children's first visit to
Narnia together, who does Peter decide should
lead them?

27. Who, for a while, vowed to accompany
Reepicheep to the end of the world, before
Aslan insisted he turned back?

28. What did Shift tell the animals of Narnia: that he
was a man who had been trapped in Underland
for ages, that he was a man who was hundreds
of years old, or that he was a man who came
from the Western Wilds?

29. Who was the last of the four children to see
Aslan in *Prince Caspian*?

30. Who became Eustace's most constant companion
on Dragon Island: Edmund, Rhince or
Reepicheep?

31. In *The Silver Chair*, on what creatures' backs
did Jill and Eustace ride to Cair Paravel?

32. Who was dressed in fawn skin with vine leaves
in his curly hair: Bacchus, Silenus, Miraz or
Caspian?

33. Who started aiming giant rocks at a cairn near
to Jill, Eustace and Puddleglum?

34. Which one of the following was not a member of Prince Rabadash's forces: Anradin, Azrooh, Ashkash, or Corradin?

35. In *The Voyage of the Dawn Treader*, who tried to write out his story in the sand on the beach but could not manage it?

36. What fruit did Trumpkin wrap in bear meat to make a delicious roasted dinner?

37. Who held Digory's hand as he held Jadis's heel?

38. What was the name of the island, beginning with the letter G, which the *Dawn Treader* had sailed past before encountering Eustace and the others?

39. In *The Last Battle*, who was the best at navigating by the stars: Jill, Eustace or King Tirian?

40. Which story did Rishda Tarkaan appear in: *The Silver Chair*, *The Last Battle*, or *The Voyage of the Dawn Treader*?

41. In *The Silver Chair*, what sort of animal was Glimfeather?

42. Which creature, beginning with the letter F, had small horns on their head?

43. Which doctor was a half-dwarf?

44. Where would you find Beruna: Archenland, Calormen, or Narnia?

45. In *The Silver Chair*, what colour was the great serpent which stung the hand of Prince Rilian's mother?

46. What was the name of the island, beginning with the letter T, which the *Dawn Treader* had sailed past before encountering Eustace and the others?

47. In *The Horse and his Boy*, who promises never to hurt cats again, after one keeps him company?

48. What was the first creature Peter battled against in *The Lion, the Witch and the Wardrobe*?

49. In *The Last Battle*, were the bear and the boar on King Tirian's side or on the enemy's side?

50. What is Doorn: a dwarf, a mermaid, or an island?

HARD
QUESTIONS

1. Which talking animal accompanied Caspian and the children onto the island of Felimath?

2. What was the name of the city where Polly and Digory first met the Queen?

3. Whose photograph in his study did Uncle Andrew show Digory moments after Polly had disappeared?

4. In *The Silver Chair*, what two words were the message of Jill's dream on her first night in Harfang?

5. In *The Last Battle*, what, according to Rishda, would happen to the unicorn if it surrendered?

6. What was the name of the Tarkheena that Aravis spotted being carried in a litter by four slaves in Tashbaan?

7. What group of islands did the *Dawn Treader* first land at?

8. What pleasant nickname was Rabadash given when he became Tisroc?

9. Can you name either of Duffle's brothers?

10. Whose godmother was Mrs Lefay?

11. What was the original name of the first horse that spoke in *The Magician's Nephew*?

12. What was the name of the Captain of the Secret Police in Narnia?

13. What is the name given to the woods which have grown up around the ruins of Cair Paravel castle?

14. Prince Caspian met three Old Narnia characters, after falling off his horse. Which wanted to kill him with its knife?

15. Who did Coriakin ask for an account of the entire voyage of the *Dawn Treader*?

16. What is the name of Prince Rilian's horse?

17. Who explained how they were going to kill themselves with their brother's dagger, before a talking horse saved them?

18. What sort of creature shaved Aslan's mane?

19. Who did the Warder of Underland take Puddleglum, Eustace and Jill to see?

20. Belisar and Uvilas were shot by arrows in a hunting party – but by whose orders?

21. How many crescents does the Tarkaan, Anradin, first offer to buy Shasta?

22. Can you name either of Miraz's Lords who conspire to get Miraz to fight Peter?

23. Who knocked a policeman to the ground with part of a lamp post?

24. What was the name of the Professor's housekeeper?

25. Who is described in *The Lion, the Witch and the Wardrobe* as son of the Emperor-beyond-the-sea?

26. What was the first name of Digory's mother?

27. What happened to Queen Prunaprismia, which meant that Prince Caspian's life was in danger?

28. In *The Silver Chair*, King Caspian set sail for what group of islands?

29. In *Prince Caspian*, who forced Lucy down to the floor to avoid arrows from Miraz's soldiers?

30. The first time Digory and Polly met a certain character, she was wearing an apron and there were soapsuds on her hands – who was she?

31. What was the name of the river Jill and Eustace had to cross to reach Ettinsmoor?

32. What sort of creature drove the White Witch's sledge?

33. What did Peter become known as, once he became King of Narnia?

34. What item does Rumblebuffin ask for after he demolished the towers and gates of the White Witch's castle?

35. Bree says that crossing the Winding Arrow river has taken them into which land?

36. In their first visit to Narnia, what was the first bird that the four Pevensie children saw?

37. In *The Last Battle*, who did Lucy and the others first meet after swimming up the waterfall?

38. In *Prince Caspian*, how many living things were in the boat the children first spied from the island containing the ruins of Cair Paravel?

39. In *Prince Caspian*, what was the name of the chief mole?

40. What was the full title of the hermit that Shasta and Aravis met shortly after they had entered Archenland?

41. In *The Last Battle*, who was the leader of the group of dwarfs who shot at both Tirian's forces and Rishda's?

42. What was the name of the raven from Narnia that Shasta meets in Tashbaan?

43. What sort of magic do Aslan and the Queen talk about at the Stone Table?

44. How many horsemen was Prince Rabadash taking for his attack on Archenland and Narnia?

45. In *Prince Caspian*, the ruined building on the island turned out to be what castle?

46. In *The Magician's Nephew*, who, according to Aslan, are the only two characters in Narnia to have known grief?

47. What creature did Doctor Cornelius say had betrayed Prince Caspian?

48. In *The Lion, the Witch and the Wardrobe*, what did the Queen and her dwarf hide as, when the animals sent by Aslan arrived to rescue Edmund?

49. What group of creatures did Trufflehunter and the two dwarfs first lead Prince Caspian to meet?

50. When Lucy couldn't sleep at Glasswater Creek, she could see three constellations of stars. Can you name them?

EASY
ANSWERS

1. CS Lewis
2. A lion
3. Polly, Digory
4. A wardrobe
5. Uncle Albert
6. Four
7. King Caspian
8. A dwarf
9. Susan, Peter and Edmund
10. Seven

11. *The Magician's Nephew*
12. Winter
13. Aslan's Quest
14. No
15. *Prince Caspian*
16. Purple
17. A donkey
18. *The Magician's Nephew*
19. No
20. Archenland

21. The Ice Queen
22. Shasta
23. Giants
24. True
25. Narnia

26. One
27. A gloomy personality
28. Ashley
29. *The Last Battle*
30. Snowy

31. Tirian
32. By oars
33. Calormen
34. Digory
35. Yellow
36. Susan
37. No
38. Her wrist
39. Peter
40. A dwarf

41. Aslan
42. Scrubb
43. Peter
44. Edmund
45. Corin
46. False
47. *The Dawn Treader*
48. *The Silver Chair*
49. Nuts
50. Wig-wams

MEDIUM ANSWERS

QUIZ 1

1. Trumpkin
2. Tumnus
3. Cair Paravel
4. Queen Polly
5. A double peak
6. A hedgehog
7. India
8. A sofa
9. Prince Caspian
10. A dozen

11. Some grapes
12. Felimath
13. A tree
14. Edmund
15. Brandy
16. The Second World War
17. Guinea pigs
18. The Hermit's house
19. A bat
20. Tumnus

21. Susan
22. A flute
23. Ivy
24. Prince Caspian
25. King Frank
26. Digory

27. King Lune
28. A knife (a dagger)
29. Archenland
30. A charwoman and a duchess

31. Apples
32. Eustace
33. He will turn back into an ass
34. A robin
35. Prince Caspian
36. Lucy
37. A mound
38. An umbrella
39. Copper, chestnut
40. The Hall of Ice

41. Mr Tumnus
42. Dwarfs
43. Narnia
44. A jackal's cry
45. The Autumn Feast
46. Susan
47. Nearly 30 days
48. High Ruler of Narnia
49. They are too old
50. A wolf

QUIZ 2

1. Two
2. Sadness
3. Edmund
4. Caspian
5. Salt mines
6. Roonwit
7. Shasta
8. Coriakin
9. Edmund
10. Shift

11. A hedgehog
12. Red
13. His hand
14. *The Horse and his Boy*
15. A slave girl
16. Susan
17. Queen of Narnia
18. Edmund
19. Jill
20. Eustace

21. Peter
22. Wells
23. Trumpkin
24. Jill
25. Prince Rilian

26. Doctor Cornelius
27. Jadis
28. Edmund
29. A stag
30. At a railway station

31. A spear
32. Caspian
33. A private cinema
34. Two clasps
35. Attack the sea serpent
    with a sword
36. Two
37. Aslan's How
38. A ship
39. False
40. A horn

41. By oars
42. The Duke of Galma
43. A fisherman
44. Lucy
45. Glasswater Creek
46. Uncle Andrew
47. Edmund, Lucy and Eustace
48. Green
49. Pug
50. His uncle, Miraz

QUIZ 3

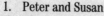

1. Peter and Susan
2. Lasaraleen
3. It has regrown
4. Two miles
5. Jill
6. Glimfeather
7. The Dancing Lawn
8. Caspian
9. Bury them
10. On the beach

11. The Western Wild
12. Wimbleweather
13. An axe
14. Half a pint
15. Roasted goat
16. Aslan
17. Lilies
18. A red lion
19. *The Voyage of the Dawn Treader*
20. Mixed

21. Fish
22. Less rude and annoying
23. The Witch's house
24. Harfang
25. Bigger and more red

26. Miraz
27. Peter
28. Nikabrik, Trumpkin, Doctor Cornelius, Trufflehunter
29. A suit of armour
30. Purple

31. Turkish delight
32. The dead dragon
33. On a train
34. Bacon
35. All living things die except the one who speaks it
36. Stable Hill
37. Drums
38. Helen
39. A rabbit
40. A giant

41. Strawberry
42. A lion
43. Mr Tumnus
44. Miraz
45. Peter
46. False
47. A lettuce
48. Edmund
49. His left arm
50. A rapier (a sword)

QUIZ 4

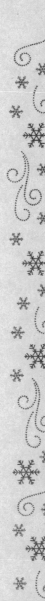

1. A faun
2. Golden
3. King of Archenland
4. The Trolls
5. Lord Argoz, Lord Revilian, Lord Mavramorn
6. Fish course
7. Father Christmas
8. Corin and Shasta
9. It cracked in two
10. True

11. Andrew
12. Lucy and Susan
13. Dufflepuds
14. Puddleglum
15. Rishda
16. Lord Rhoop
17. Cair Paravel
18. Mrs Macready
19. A mole
20. River Rush

21. Unicorns, deer
22. Aslan
23. A ship
24. Blue
25. Golg

26. Underland
27. A hansom cab
28. Narnia
29. Toast
30. A blazer and a sweater

31. Tarkheena
32. The talking dogs
33. The Great Central Tower
34. His tail
35. Scrubb
36. Peter and Edmund
37. A red squirrel
38. A compass
39. One
40. The Queen (Jadis)

41. The *Dawn Treader*'s shadow
42. Feed the crew
43. Three
44. Shasta
45. Polly Plummer
46. True
47. Trumpkin
48. One mile
49. Lucy
50. Royal blood

QUIZ 5

1. Ketterley
2. His dagger
3. Mr Tumnus
4. Drinian
5. Fresh dragon
6. It had been slashed into shreds
7. A mouse
8. The Queen (Jadis)
9. Lunch
10. Rabadash

11. Aslan
12. Peter
13. King Tirian
14. Prince Corin
15. Because it came from a talking stag
16. A friend
17. Lucy
18. Experiment House
19. A nightingale
20. Eustace

21. Aravis
22. 11 dwarfs
23. Caldron Pool
24. Peter

25. Cair Paravel
26. Archery, swimming
27. A guinea pig
28. Four
29. The Tombs of the Ancient Kings
30. Mrs Beaver

31. It got bigger
32. A dozen
33. Aslan's footprint
34. Red (scarlet)
35. An owl
36. Part of the roof
37. The Fords of Beruna
38. Uncle Andrew's study
39. Spring
40. Queen Susan the Gentle

41. Statues
42. Seven
43. A dragon
44. Jewel the unicorn
45. True
46. At the Stone Table
47. Crimson
48. Fine robes
49. Hide and seek
50. The river-god

QUIZ 6

1. Stable Hill
2. A cat
3. Edmund
4. A statue of a lion
5. The warthog
6. Unpleasant
7. Red dwarfs
8. Dogs
9. Calormen
10. The Great Snow Dance

11. Lucy
12. An oak tree
13. A prophet
14. Reepicheep
15. Four
16. A battering ram
17. Narnia
18. Doctor Cornelius
19. Jill
20. Duffle

21. Stable Hill
22. Lucy, Edmund, Eustace and Reepicheep
23. Eustace
24. Duffers
25. Wimbleweather

26. White
27. Between two hills
28. Prince Corin
29. 12
30. Susan

31. Susan
32. Rubies
33. A punt
34. The snow began to thaw
35. Three o'clock
36. A city
37. Trumpkin
38. Mrs Lefay
39. Digory
40. Shasta (Prince Cor)

41. Spectacles and a moustache
42. Eustace
43. The court of Archenland
44. An ancient Queen of Narnia
45. His mother
46. Marsh-wiggles
47. Edmund
48. Mr Tumnus
49. Lucy
50. Almost no time at all

QUIZ 7

1. Dwarfs
2. Delighted
3. Edmund
4. Goat's milk
5. Peter and Susan
6. Jill
7. May
8. Aslan
9. As a child
10. About a third

11. Never
12. Two
13. The Tisroc's
14. Red
15. Queen Jadis
16. False
17. Shift
18. Emeth
19. Prince Rilian
20. A dwarf

21. Reepicheep
22. Chervy
23. True
24. Hard-boiled egg, cheese, paste

25. The courtyard
26. Mr Tumnus
27. Lucy and Susan
28. Marsh-wiggle
29. The Queen
30. A beaver

31. A thicket
32. Jill Pole
33. North
34. *The Last Battle*
35. Mr and Mrs Beaver
36. Almost to his knees
37. Narnia
38. Red
39. A tiger
40. Two

41. Loneliness
42. Blue
43. Lucy
44. Trumpkin
45. Chess
46. His club
47. Nikabrik
48. Peter
49. Her horn
50. Puddleglum

QUIZ 8

1. Lord Bern
2. Prince Rabadash
3. A giant serpent
4. *The Lion, the Witch and the Wardrobe*
5. Peter
6. Ramandu
7. Shift
8. Rilian
9. Rubies
10. Prince Corin

11. Gold crowns
12. Wood-people
13. Two mothballs
14. The Stone Table
15. Narrowhaven
16. Sea horses
17. Ahoshta
18. The Hall of Images
19. Eustace
20. An albatross

21. A lamp post
22. Her brother's armour
23. Purple
24. Bears
25. The Great Oak
26. Corin

27. Tashlan
28. Digory, Polly
29. Edmund
30. The eagle

31. Doctor Cornelius
32. Fire flowers
33. The Tisroc
34. Lucy
35. The Great Sea Serpent
36. Trumpkin
37. A cat
38. Blacksmith
39. A castle
40. Digory

41. Rhindon
42. Calormen
43. Digory's
44. The dwarf and Edmund
45. Wimbleweather the giant and Glenstorm
46. Logic
47. Figs, pomegranate, orange, melon
48. Stale bread
49. A Calormen soldier
50. Peter, Edmund, Lucy, Susan, Digory, Polly, Eustace and Jill

QUIZ 9

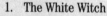

1. The White Witch
2. Clarence
3. Panthers, leopards
4. Rishda
5. The Cabby and Polly
6. Mrs Beaver
7. Golden
8. Eustace
9. Yellow and green
10. A great war-horse

11. Doctor Cornelius
12. Digory
13. A donkey
14. An electric torch
15. A horse
16. Rabadash
17. Gwendolen
18. His feet
19. Puddleglum
20. A scimitar

21. Cair Paravel
22. *The Last Battle*
23. The Stone Table (Aslan's How)
24. Jill
25. Edmund

26. Cair Paravel
27. Pole
28. The box room
29. Rishda
30. Aslan

31. Hwin
32. King Caspian
33. True
34. The Cabby's wife
35. His horn
36. Deathwater Island
37. Loyal to him
38. Lucy
39. Less rude and dangerous
40. Five

41. No (he had been in other worlds but not the land of Narnia)
42. The legs of a goat
43. The two girls
44. Six
45. The jeweller
46. Aslan
47. Janet
48. A fur coat
49. A marsh-wiggle
50. A wolf

QUIZ 10

1. Doctor Cornelius
2. Eustace Scrubb
3. Peter
4. A string of pearls
5. Buried it in the garden
6. Edmund
7. Fourth
8. Ahoshta
9. Nikabrik, Trumpkin and Prince Caspian
10. Queen Susan

11. A Wer-Wolf
12. Jewel
13. A ring
14. Governor Gumpas
15. A giant
16. Bree
17. The Queen
18. Lantern Waste
19. Pack them so they could be sold
20. A spare dress

21. Lasaraleen's groom
22. At peace
23. A year
24. Lucy

25. Aslan
26. The Queen
27. Her sister
28. True
29. A hare
30. Dozens of reed beds

31. A cave
32. The lamp post
33. No
34. Wipe it clean
35. Lord Drinian
36. Atlantis
37. Leopards
38. Corin
39. False
40. Apples

41. Trufflehunter
42. Aslan
43. A lamp post
44. Trumpkin
45. Pattertwig
46. A lion
47. Peter and Edmund
48. Tumnus
49. An apple tree
50. Mallard, Man, Marsh-wiggle

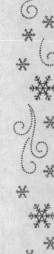

QUIZ 11

1. A harp
2. Aslan
3. Six marshals
4. Jill Pole
5. Nellie
6. Polly
7. Camillo
8. Aslan
9. Susan
10. Two

11. Peter
12. The White Witch
13. Seven
14. King Tirian
15. Prince Caspian's
16. North
17. Stars
18. Gnomes
19. Glenstorm
20. False

21. Trufflehunter
22. Prince Corin
23. Green
24. Six
25. It was not salt water, it was fresh water.

26. Cor
27. Sarah
28. Eustace
29. Curved and sharp
30. Game pie

31. Harfang
32. A bunch of keys
33. Red
34. Black
35. Edmund
36. Dwarfs
37. Snow
38. The Queen
39. An ass (a donkey)
40. Rubies

41. A dwarf
42. Eustace
43. The missing prince
44. Slave traders
45. A handkerchief
46. Doctor Cornelius
47. Centaurs
48. Lions
49. Trumpkin
50. The Queen of Underland

QUIZ 12

1. *The Horse and his Boy*
2. Susan
3. High Treason
4. Sulky
5. Mr and Mrs Beaver's
6. Cair Paravel
7. The letter E
8. The Queen
9. His father
10. Tarva and Alambil

11. Lucy
12. True
13. Poggin
14. Reepicheep
15. Clive Staples
16. Bree and Hwin
17. A mole
18. Uncle Andrew
19. One
20. Mrs Lefay

21. A jackdaw
22. One
23. A wolf
24. Four
25. His nurse

26. Lucy's handkerchief
27. Trumpkin
28. Brother and sister
29. Mr Beaver
30. A lamb

31. Lucy
32. By ship
33. The Bull-Elephant
34. Edmund and Lucy
35. Lord Protector
36. Digory
37. The beavers'
38. Aslan
39. Jingling bells
40. Drug a maid

41. Grass
42. In the wardrobe
43. Stonefoot
44. Down the Tisroc's mines
45. The Queen
46. Sir Peter Wolf's-Bane
47. Badgers
48. A steam train
49. Silver
50. Six

QUIZ 13

1. Uncle Andrew
2. Narnians
3. Polly
4. A satchel
5. Queen Jadis
6. Satyrs
7. A dragon
8. Moles
9. Four
10. Old Father Time

11. A lion
12. Puzzle
13. At the Stone Table
14. Edmund
15. Edmund
16. A donkey
17. Nikabrik
18. A red dwarf
19. Susan
20. Three

21. Trout
22. The Witch
23. Aslan's How, Cair Paravel, Lantern Waste
24. Digory
25. Edmund

26. Eustace Scrubb
27. Bree
28. Fledge
29. The Tisroc
30. Two

31. Pattertwig
32. The Dancing Lawn
33. Puzzle
34. A messenger
35. Five
36. A toffee
37. The Stone Table
38. The Stone Table
39. Caspian the Conqueror
40. *The Dawn Treader*

41. A musical instrument
42. Aravis
43. A teacher
44. Prince Rilian
45. Eustace
46. Caspian (King Caspian the Tenth)
47. Puzzle the donkey
48. Spears
49. North
50. Currant buns

QUIZ 14

1. World's End
2. Edmund
3. Against them
4. The *Dawn Treader*
5. Eustace
6. The centaurs
7. Queen Helen
8. Mrs Beaver
9. Digory
10. A dog-fox

11. Reepicheep
12. Doctor Cornelius
13. Jill
14. A thorn
15. Chief of Narnia's Realms
16. Tash
17. Deathwater Island
18. The Queen (Jadis)
19. Peter
20. A green ribbon

21. Overworld creatures
22. Red
23. The Black Knight
24. Roonwit
25. The Great Central Tower

26. Puddleglum
27. Emeth
28. Eustace and Jill
29. Jadis and Uncle Andrew
30. Trufflehunter

31. The bear
32. Harold
33. The Queen (Jadis)
34. Eustace
35. Three
36. Alberta
37. Aslan
38. Cheese, oatcakes, butter
39. Feldar
40. King Tirian

41. Dwarfs
42. Uncle Andrew
43. Cambridge
44. Dragons, giant lizards
45. Ham sandwiches
46. Roast pheasant
47. *Prince Caspian*
48. Edmund
49. Uncle Andrew
50. 40 crescents

QUIZ 15

1. Moles
2. Edmund
3. A lion
4. The dwarfs
5. Iron
6. A castle
7. A badger
8. Edmund
9. Farsight
10. Reepicheep

11. King Tirian's
12. Sledge
13. Manatu
14. False
15. Aslan
16. Edmund
17. Three
18. The south of Narnia
19. Reepicheep
20. Red

21. A goose
22. The River Rush
23. A sledge
24. 10 dwarf archers
25. An island

26. Blue cheese
27. A half-dwarf
28. Goldwater Island
29. Edmund
30. Badgers

31. Lord Rhoop
32. Four
33. In trees
34. Against them
35. A horse
36. Dinner
37. Crescents
38. Dorset
39. British Railways
40. Puddleglum

41. The railway station
42. Aravis
43. Anvard
44. The tower in Lantern Waste
45. None
46. Her wand
47. His nurse
48. Shift
49. Susan
50. Bristol

QUIZ 16

1. The magic horn (of Queen Susan)
2. Susan
3. His father's
4. A wardrobe
5. His ear
6. Aslan
7. Aravis
8. West
9. More than 10 years
10. The stables

11. The Black Knight
12. Four
13. Trumpkin
14. Lilith
15. Prince Rabadash
16. Trufflehunter
17. Half an hour before
18. Mice, moles and rabbits
19. Aravis
20. Bree

21. Dear Little Friend
22. Less evil
23. The dwarfs
24. Queen Lucy

25. Old Father Time
26. Prince Cor
27. Telmarines
28. With his knees
29. A sword, a shield
30. Peter, Edmund, Trumpkin

31. Uncle Andrew
32. Eels
33. To hide a mad wife
34. The Head Faun
35. Send him to sleep
36. Red
37. Puzzle
38. Lucy and Susan
39. Emeralds
40. Old Father Time

41. A lion
42. Reepicheep
43. Tashbaan
44. Susan
45. The Witch (Queen Jadis)
46. 16 steps
47. Squirrels
48. The White Witch
49. Telmarines
50. Dwarfs

QUIZ 17

1. Honey
2. A great lord
3. The Chamber of Instruments
4. Stable Hill
5. Three
6. Dwarfs
7. Father Christmas
8. Digory
9. Edmund
10. Shaved their beards, wore high-heeled shoes, pretended to be men

11. Prince Rilian
12. The top floor
13. Reepicheep
14. The nurse
15. Corin
16. Fruit
17. A mattress
18. Edmund's
19. Ginger
20. Jewel

21. Digory
22. The scullery
23. An owl

24. 7th August
25. King Gale
26. Between 20 and 25
27. Birds
28. Jill
29. Snowflake
30. Coriakin

31. King Lune
32. Edmund
33. Lantern Waste
34. Edmund and Lucy
35. The Shadowlands
36. For them
37. Peter and Edmund
38. Edmund
39. Uncle Andrew
40. Old Father Time

41. The Southern Mountains
42. Mr Tumnus
43. A knife
44. A helmet
45. Yellow
46. Pittencream
47. Eustace
48. Peridan
49. The White Stag
50. A lamp post

QUIZ 18

1. Susan
2. A kill
3. Prince Rabadash
4. Edmund
5. A knife
6. Noon
7. Lucy
8. Lord Bar
9. Caspian
10. Mr and Mrs Beaver

11. Aslan
12. Destrier
13. The Queen
14. Queen Jadis (The White Witch)
15. Three
16. Edmund
17. Calormen
18. The Summer holidays
19. Reepicheep
20. Tash

21. Ghosts
22. Mr Beaver
23. Jill Pole
24. Lucy

25. A mandolin
26. Mice
27. Milk
28. Over a half full
29. The Spear-Head
30. Ginger beer

31. A penknife
32. Coriakin
33. Prince Rabadash's army
34. A water rat
35. Fur coats
36. Uncle Andrew
37. His tail
38. Bows and arrows
39. Uncle Andrew
40. Reepicheep

41. The dragon's cave
42. Fledge
43. Two
44. Both
45. Aunt Letty
46. A humming sound
47. Jill
48. Roonwit
49. Eustace's
50. Jill

QUIZ 19

1. King Tirian
2. Susan and Lucy
3. Mouthpiece of Aslan
4. Peter
5. Polly
6. Aslan
7. A rabbit
8. The Great Woods
9. Digory's
10. Uncle Andrew

11. Susan
12. Shasta
13. Three
14. Shift
15. The Cabby
16. Her bureau
17. Jill
18. A gold bell
19. Jewel and King Tirian
20. Father Christmas

21. Their pockets
22. The Cabby
23. The Wood Between the Worlds
24. Eustace and Jill
25. Brownish dye from skin

26. Lucy
27. Caspian
28. A man who was hundreds of years old
29. Susan
30. Reepicheep

31. Centaurs
32. Bacchus
33. The giants
34. Ashkash
35. Eustace
36. Apple
37. Polly
38. Galma
39. Jill
40. *The Last Battle*

41. An owl
42. Fauns
43. Doctor Cornelius
44. Narnia
45. Green
46. Terebinthea
47. Shasta
48. A wolf
49. On King Tirian's side
50. An island

HARD
ANSWERS

1. Reepicheep
2. Charn
3. Mrs Lefay
4. Under Me
5. It would have its horn sawn off and then work, pulling a cart
6. Lasaraleen
7. The Lone Islands
8. Rabadash the Peacemaker
9. Bricklethumb, Rogin
10. Uncle Andrew

11. Strawberry
12. Maugrim
13. The Black Woods
14. Nikabrik
15. Drinian
16. Coalblack
17. Aravis
18. An ogre
19. The Queen of the Deep Realm
20. Miraz

21. 15
22. Lord Glozelle, Lord Sopespian
23. Queen Jadis
24. Mrs Macready

25. Aslan
26. Mabel
27. She gave birth to a son
28. Seven Isles
29. Trumpkin
30. The Cabby's wife

31. The Shribble
32. A dwarf
33. King Peter the Magnificent
34. A handkerchief
35. Archenland
36. A robin
37. Reepicheep
38. Three
39. Lilygloves
40. The Hermit of the Southern March

41. Griffle
42. Sallowpad
43. Deep Magic
44. 200
45. Cair Paravel
46. He (Aslan) and Digory
47. His horse, Destrier
48. A tree stump and a boulder
49. The Three Bulgy Bears
50. The Ship, the Hammer, the Leopard